T0380251

ANOINTED
AND
APPOINTED

Timothy Green

AuthorHouse™ UK
1663 Liberty Drive
Bloomington, IN 47403 USA
www.authorhouse.co.uk
UK TFN: 0800 0148641 (Toll Free inside the UK)
UK Local: 02036 956322 (+44 20 3695 6322 from outside the UK)

Because of the dynamic nature of the Internet, any web addresses or links contained in this book may have changed
since publication and may no longer be valid. The views expressed in this work are solely those of the author and do not
necessarily reflect the views of the publisher, and the publisher hereby disclaims any responsibility for them.

Any people depicted in stock imagery provided by Getty Images are models,
and such images are being used for illustrative purposes only.
Certain stock imagery © Getty Images.

This book is printed on acid-free paper.

ISBN: 978-1-7283-7626-4 (sc)
ISBN: 978-1-7283-7627-1 (e)

Print information available on the last page.

Published by AuthorHouse 25/10/2022

authorHOUSE®

Anointed and Appointed
Timothy Green

Africa

You are taunted and laughed at;
your military is not ready for attack,
and your leaders always hold back
from giving.

Still, you are loved,
and the children of yours grow well.
Many thanks for little things.
Oh, Africa, you are in my heart.

Very dry and hot, no coverage of any kind.
The lions lie in wait
for their meal on no plate.
But we give to you
to see you through,
but it should be more.

Your children enjoy such simple things
and thankful they are for every bite.
You are the kite that sets us free,
kindly given to all who love me.

Coming across your open space,
I look forward to meeting your face
and sensing your courageous heart
that goes on regardless.

The world doesn't want you to be a burden,
but I am certain that my diversion
will matter when it comes to be.
Courtesy shown for home-grown talent—
and richly invited I feel.
Hearts of wool and wills of steel.

Lord, you are with us, right at the wheel.
Kneeling and asking of your supply.
Never denied; you are my free mind.
Free rides for us.

Anointed and Appointed

My last days have been so free.
No longer in disagreement,
several feelings don't coexist.
My very sores were my cover.
A handsome man
coming out to see the world.
Kindly, I became her man.
Plans are there to be made;
maps are old but worth their weight.

Anointed one of my choice,
you are one to project my voice.
You chose this path; see it through.
Turning to you for inspiration
gives me the power to achieve.
Believe me when I say,
'Jesus, I want it your way.'
Suggest me a song to play.
Jesus, I need to pray and play.
To this day I barely know
of the sorrow of years ago.
Delight in me, and you shall be
happy and full of dexterity,
certain to carry your weight.

As I Dine

Purposefully rectified, as my landlady would say.
Defined moments, we go out to play
all of the days and all of the nights.
Politely outspoken as I dine with peers.
'Twas years since I tasted my food.
Politely lingers just out of reach.
Nose turning to your word,
and my tongue slurring out of sync.
Bring me my food; I want to exude my defence.
I watch over you out of my lens.
Burdens and weights add to my haste,
wasting no time to fill you out.
I fill my needs with your words.
Is it real when people say you are healed?
It feels real to me.

Just like a ripened pear—
sweet and tasty and slippery and wet.
And when consumed, it needs a dispatch.
Hatching a plan to be a part of this land—
sandy shores and windy beaches.
Furrows in land; the sun keeps still
as we enjoy our picnic, our water distilled.
Those wretched fish that swarm and sting—
no more swimming in Dover's Sea.
But I shall have my share of Christ's eternity.
Deep in understanding and casually landing on earth.

Shallow the tides to swim against.
My yoke is carried and shared from time to time.

Brilliantly in white and purity divine.
What's mine is yours, and your love is mine.
Keep digging and wedge out those mines,
the ones that go off or are dangerously close.
Ration packs carried for nourishment
are used to dish out punishment,
but not always.

We pray for peace and wait upon you,
delivering your Word to the less fortunate.
The life-affirming Word that carries weight.
Morning comes but not too late.
Figure this out before the night comes.
It is the way.
Nightly figures rinsed in ambition.
A rainy day would help.
Casting out fears, the nets are cleared,
and when it gets to us,
the food is made to our tastes.
A mere hesitation, and the plate is laid.
Full of colour, we look forward.
The whole experience struck me like a velvet glove.
As we turn to you for your lovely smile,
come with me, and run the extra mile

As I Wait

I lie in wait for my virtuous child,
the one I care for as I chew the bark.
It is a great way to be
as I search for your sea of reflection.
What you see in me I happily agree.
I need to grow even more, so I have.
Laughing at the wind and smiling
as the ships come in
to talk of their adventures.
Advancing beyond pace, you come strangely
in from the misty air that clamoured for you.
Your watch now, and don't be late.
Keep your eyes open, and watch what you eat.

It is all very simple;
come into my holy presence,
where *doubt* isn't a word, and love is heard most.
Feeling my way towards your shore,
the cure is at hand; it is almost 4:00 p.m.
Early or late, I cannot comment
on the state of that stately vessel.
Coming into mooring so early in the dawning
put me almost in a state of reflection.
Reflecting on the night's dream.
Keep me dry is what I ask as I sing.
Bring me my parrot, my stick, and watch.

You came to me as a friend does,
a new friend every time.
Such is our family in Christ.
Most heighty heights can make you flap,
with wagging and flailing arms,
in wait of an attack that never comes.
I don't know all their names.

Assured

Because of the ways of the world,
I cannot send you a child or a girl.
Calamities are not meant for them.
Your gift is often to soften the wake,
making all the difference when a pence is shared.
Commence the dig as we wait for peace.
Look for water at the watering hole.
My methods to stop devouring my children
as famine and illness take place.
We care to say we shall not have it that way,
taught and raised to be sharers.
Deterring my mission to go out there;
the flight would be such a strain.
Animals run freely untamed;
snakes willing to kill and maim,
the jackals and hyenas ready to take
what is yours.
But the worst crime would be to see
my poor sisters and brothers in adversity,
without food or shelter
or clothes on their backs.
I need to do something more to stop the attacks,
to share my experiences and knowledge of better.
The snow that falls, the careful weather,
untethered to the ways of the poor.
We have lots of food and drink in store.
I need to and should share more.

So assuredly I say to you,
'Son, you shall never be poor.
Just open the door for others to see
the wonderful future for those who love me.
Knock, and it will be opened
as I motion towards the sea.
You shall have more; I will show you.
Complete love and, to my youth,
complete and utter devotion.
Motions towards the plagues and illness.
You need to do something,
and it has to be big.'

At 9:25

It is the end of the day.
The shift and shifting sands away,
forcing their tiresome angles.
Shingles and sand mix at my beach,
where writers seek their communion,
moving in time with my divinity.
I pity the lost and scared.
For them I have prepared a way
to display their own veiled eyes.
Surprised to see me lying down
as I pity their lack of ground.
I sound into the nightly air.
It was 9:25 p.m. Remember it?
When we would prepare our day?
Come to me, and feel the way I do.
It's up to you, the way you go.
We can cut through the rain and snow,
just like the globe in rubble.
I sift through it to see the gold.
The ones who enfold my true faith—
those souls who knew nothing
but followed me regardless—
will be taken away from distress.

Upstairs

I declare their notions of potions,
correcting and recognising my space.
Tasting your rightful place of comfort.
Watching you as you sometimes stumble.
Mumbling and thinking in time with my vote.
Approval given to unleavened bread.
Suggesting a place to be upstairs.
Weeping as I count my starts.
Using and abusing my very heart.
I start to depart to my ways.
Freed and new seeds sown for you.
Newness every day, and I say unto you,
'The public voted you in,
so begin to live in your blessings,
nesting your young to grow them strong.'
Wrongs corrected, you belong to me.
No anger in you or plots or waves.
Simply saying to my love, 'You are bought.
I paid it all for you to be with me,
like going upstairs to reveal your gift.'
I cannot wait any longer; this is my goal.
I cannot hide my sides, hands, or nails.
Feet to take the weight.
Upstairs, the rejoicing is made.
Laying of hands to begin your healing.
Teething like a toddler.
Shoulder to shoulder, we wait to debate.

Crushing our enemies, we say to them, 'Leave.'
Retrieving ourselves, speaking in tonal height.
Light in my pocket, I serve up well.
I come to you satisfied for my life
And all its elegance and splendour.
Casting no shadows as we wait.
Troubles gone and elated.
Sweating and pain surrendered to you.
Placing your hand on my heart,
nurturing me and giving a fair start to finish.

Sometimes

Casually I say to thine heart,
'Please do not depart from me;
my knees are week and somewhat giddy.'
Our truth relies on truth.
It is a wonder how we keep our youth
soothing my stages of exaggerated anxiety,
calmly wondering, *Is this to be?*
In all sincerity, my craft is my pathway;
such honesty is hard to find in this day.
Country miles can be run in the mud.
But I say to you while you understand,
take care of the one who grants you her plans,
a second look undertook, just in case.
Troubles all removed and erased from memory,
this story comes with a wish as we talk
that you do remember what you are taught.
The battle is over now, so reach out for me.
I will devour all sorcery.
See me as I am, where the plans are grand;
not of this land, I planned the days and nights.
All I see now are my open plans to take up,
take up your mat, and walk in prosperity.
Do not worry of what is said to you.
In all truth, they are lies, and they don't matter.
But they do matter, and we struggle to see sense
in of all the ones I have witnessed.
I see your strong and courageous heart.

Your will is good, and your ways are gentle,
mentally sound, and found pure and righteous.
I enjoy these nights and days in prayer.
How lovely to see ya.
And your name is rightly so praised and worthy.
I honour you with my heart and my tongue.
Even your morsels are enough to live on.

Beyond

What I see and bear are not the same things.
Pages are blurred, but still I sing my song.
We belong to our master, sound and joy.
At this very moment, poised to deliver the mail,
sense is misguided when I follow my tail.
Courteously, I do not fail to deliver.
Cross-membered beams seem to hold
the unwanted treasure seeming beyond measure.
Careless little whispers made in the dusk.
Bring me my shield as I thrust another time;
my foes laughed, but who is laughing now
as I present my sword, somehow waging war
on a tyrant hell-bent on fury and his destruction,
corrupted and indecent, piteous and cruel?
He should have gone to school.
No more a burden, no more a threat,
My Jesus is with me and sweated for my salvation.

Blue

Your sentences befall me; curiously I say,
'Sort me out, and bring me my pay—I earned it.'
Subterranean dwellings course through me
like a desert meant for better.
Set on my goals, I search for the most.
My love, my goal, and my words of my soul.

Where is my control as I go through the storm?
Normally, it is my change-givers, but today, my seekers,
My family of believers achieving my goals.
We work together; my change is free.
Normality I see in the very distance.
Functionality brings its own rewards.
Turning to you with my sword, I swipe away fear,
nearly cutting at the flesh but reasonable skill
to tell the tale of a destiny fulfilled.
Chilled to the core as you raised the sword.
Undeterred, you fight for me.
Understanding and wisdom I send to thee.
As your freedom begins to flourish,
heart sighted burnished strength.
Length of days worry me not as I walk on through,
chewing the matter, refusing to scatter.
My hat I keep with me for those hot sunny days
that blaze at the skin and ruins it within.

Calling Me

When I slip, it is not a fall.
When you stare, you befall me.
Literary injection of pace,
picking me up for the race.
Common to my conclusion,
my life-giver no illusion.
My fruits are from my Lord.
As I cross swords with my enemy,
my Lord gently says to me,
'This is my battle, so let me fight
for you have a home to protect.
Don't take it all on your head
as I lead to triumphant battle,
rattling them until they shatter,
what is the matter?'
Calling me are my sea friends.
You surfers are courteous to show
what it is all about.

It is not what I do that counts.
It is who I am with,
shouting my name everywhere.
Come to my Lord, cast a care
sweating out in those clothes.

You chose to follow quick on your
toes.

Canoe

You, me, and the canoe—
a true perfect match.
Where the sun directs our paths,
paths waged against this diluted land,
bring your energy, and the sand
handles my growth in every way.
Is it really poetry day?

Certainly, you cause me to believe
you are worth keeping.
In all subtlety you deploy
these royal wheels.

Skirting beyond the edge,
my canoe takes me there
as I sing and sway, push and force.
But the water takes you in an odd destination,
one we could not play for.
Seeking out your wonderous signs,
come to me in all keepers' find.
Mind the rocks and depths below.
I wish we had sails to go my way.
But yours is the rudder,
and I shall agree with the journey.
The colours, the shapes,
taking in your breath.
Misshapen oddities, wondrous in sight.

In my canoe, you have safety
as you make my way gently into the future.
Your raft is precious,
and I shall hold onto you.
You, me, and the canoe,
we rise without harm.
No alarms raised about you.

Carefree

Drizzling your flavour for me,
this serving hatch is open always.
Days so hard, such pace and display.
Oh, Lord, let's say as we pray,
'Spirited one, the one we lean on,
come and free us from this table.
The table serving cold food
and tasteless carboard.
it has been so long since
I tasted your manna fully.
but I don't worry about it.
Pease release me from negativity.
Respond to my call
because I feel nothing at all.
This life partly enjoyed,
it's such a void in my life.
I take and give thanks anyway,
but I am lacking in your ways.
The love I felt for humanity,
strained but for good reason,
detached and driven back again.
I am a tree swaying in the wind.
Some day it will flower
and bear much fruit.'

Cares

Cast them on me
as I go through life.
Amazed at you
and your treasures
you keep so close,
mostly and costly
choose to stay still.
Thrills me to keep
ahead of the pack.
No turning around,
no looking back,
Messengers riot;
I clear my way,
displays my heart.
Lonesome friend,
never depart from me.
Don't make that wrong.

Carry Me Homeward

Feeling you and the breath you receive,
you freely give your sincere beliefs.
Retrieve my hopes and cares,
and make them in line with yours.
Time is ticking away.
We have so much to say to each other.
Weathering the heavy heights,
politely calling your delights.
Come to me; I shall give you the rights
to complain and maintain your innocence.
It can rain at any time here.
The sun shines heavily within the summer years.
Clearly, there are other ways to see.
You believe me when I say I love you.
See these plans through, and you shall be strong.
Success comes, so belong to the cause.
Pause for a few moments, and ask yourself, *How,*
how can I supply your need?
As I go on bleeding onto the page,
it is a labour of love, tough enough to grow.
Knowing the line I really want to show
below the gaps we do not seep through.
Taunting but powerless to get us
thrusting your knowledge, not easily received.
Breathe into me, and you shall create love
like I do; look into me, and rest you will find.

I may be tall and kind, but sir, open my mind.
Cry my tears for me; they are too much to bear,
caring about your resolve and strength to go on.
Come on, and solve this puzzle called life.
I give you strength and a beautiful wife.

Cast No Shadow

Coasting through these words,
we cast no shadow on the earth.
Turfing out the foggy days
playing and remembering.
Semblance and order bordering
my shock at what they are ordering.
Not fast food or a table clean,
but someone who may take you to the cleaners.
A sudden passing through no faults of their own.
Clear as day what happened.
We pray for our souls to stay clean,
washed permanently with royal blood,
no blot or blemish.
Replenish our strengths and spirits;
there are ways to shine.
And you are mine to do these works,
jerking and pulling at your very heart.
But with me, you always have a head start.
No shadow formed or reaching our forms
called into action but slightly deformed.
I rise above it all,
taller than any of my adversaries.
Bring me to church for a release,
ceasing to be a worldly resident.
My home is with my Maker,
voting for my honourable president,
cementing my place amongst the stars.

Heartedly found among the strong,
tough times left behind as I carry on
purposefully and with supernatural vigour,
seeking my days of rest.
Blessings upon blessings.
I hear my call, there with you,
small in shape but large in heart.
My Saviour, come; I want to feel yours.
Plenty of time for applause.
This course of yours, I finished the race,
my purposeful notions erasing fears and doubt.
My lovely king, the greatest,
not for the faint-hearted to start this.

Casting My Cares on You

You are my skin in supple fruition.
To keep me together, that is your mission.
Not indecision, no prison for correction.
Mention the time I was in detention.

Mess up my hair; put me to the floor,
but don't scratch my records.
I think of you as I write;
form you are in, a subtle delight.
Pity the man who fights for his right
to take life and then his own.
It is he whom we see wandering the land.
No tear in his eyes and no plan for better,
letter to letter, is he really changed?
The institution believes so.

It is meant for our growth.
You may be seventy, but don't be your age,
knowing the wrongs and putting them right.
Call me late, but the night lights up
when we see a sinner repent and change
as we carry on and take our wage.
Some age before their time.
Come to me; I want to give you time.
Fortunate enough to learn to climb
as we focus on the essentials,
like learning and yearning for our Father.

Mastering the way we share,
cast my cares away from me.
Lord, take these burdens and free me.
I am only a man as I cease to be
young enough to carry on
but still delighted in an earthly song.
Belonging to me, you cannot be wrong
as we come together, a merry throng.

Catch My Breath

Unearthed are the virtues of mine
where crime is hidden amongst the storm.
Casting out my net, fruitless it seems.
Who casts into a storm?
These days it is common and real.
The realities feel pointless to me
as I search for life amongst the sea.
Plenty of fish, but jumpy and afraid.
My labour nearly killed me.
But I rose, and with all my strength
abated the woeful mess
where I dressed to impress.
Even on this vessel I yearn for power,
the power to change my life if I wish,
one to harness creativity.
But I know deep in my heart
you are the creator, and I wait.
Your ways are far above mine,
where decline is sealed and sent away.
The envelope reaches its destination
in the sea of forgetfulness.
I catch my breath in the cold wind.
It came back to me.
My life I now have is precious and loved,
my little trinkets shared.
The world, is it prepared for your return?

Many live without concern.
As we turn out in droves,
the pain goes and is once again sent
to return to sender.
Remember my title and my hook.
The book is magnificent,
worthy of a happy, loving Father.
I want to see you in a book
rather than in jail.

Celebrating My Holiday

Coursing through my veins,
I see a vending store,
the one you see secure.
I saw this and thought of you,
so I picked this one out
and remember you all,
no matter how small or tall.
The view was amazingly fresh.
I aired the speech and see freedom.
The beach and tide, I see them.
My kite I bear in the wind.
Friendly people search for me,
but I come out when I win.
The bingo was fun.
Then I began my searching wits.
Found you on the waves.
You come to me, amazed as I wave,
the state I was in as I looked.
Hooked I am on your beauty.
Curtsy shown royalty to me.
Let's celebrate and toast the queen.
Serenity found but not always seen.
Clearly you are happy.

Check My Food

My food is your food.
We share it all, no crumb wasted.
Tasting my tasty senses,
no alarm of pretence or change.
We hope to make it different,
this spiritual food we share,
declaring my stately dessert,
hurt by my answers,
showing all of life's chancers.
Angle me a little shelf
as I grow in my mental health.
Search me, see me, feel me
as I stir this pot of joy.
Boisterous noise, lavished partners.
Where are my friends as I drift,
missed by mis-education.
Conversations rationed, held close,
testing the time I give you,
making sure it's you I see.

In your grace and power,
shower me with hope and wishes.
My Lord, you are a fisher of men
as we feel a great weekend.

Climb My Rock

Sacked again as I tried the rock,
slipping slightly as I came up,
ignoring the orders to speed up,
taking a rollicking as I swig
Tabasco sauce
in climbing for your favour.
But I do not need to.
You are my Saviour I run to.
My rock and my salvation.
You are the one I try for,
causing a stir as your pores release
sweat from your brow.
Somehow you got through
as I turn to you and declare
I am God's child, and I lay it bare.
You know I am strong,
belonging to your merry throng.
Taking an honorary status
made us righteous as we complete
neat threads and heads of wires.
But they frazzled to take me higher.
You are not my hired hand,
taking control of this wondering land.
Drawn me out into the spirit
you love, I sense I am a misfit.
Boast about it, and say to the world,
'I have my Father, and I have my girl.

And that is all I need for today.'
Cast away your cares
into the ocean of forgetfulness.
Breast made of plate, rescue me
as we eat the food the poor eat.
Depleting in manna, we ask for the best.
Not just rice but a three-course meal,
feeling it on your tongue
as we sing our song for my fans.

Collectively

Do you remember when
you had it all figured out?
Had it all together without a doubt?
Cast your mind to your early ways,
The days you felt alone.
No one listened; you were not at home.
Roaming around the streets
for someone who can change
your situation and your age,
revealing you to the world,
curling up by the heater.
Many could see your plight
but watched as you fought.
I bring out the best in you,
shining as you should be known.
The adventurer
mentioned me as you played,
scoring those goals.
Man, you are ace.
Left a trace of hopeful embrace.
Come with me for an embrace.
Continue, my son, and be the best
amongst your peers; you are
guessing the right answer,
learning to pounce on it.
From it you grow and face the show.
Go on, my son, and let us grow.

Colour Me In

This chance comes in a lifetime.
Don't waste it, no crime in haste.
We wish for your very being
to be filled in with colour;
painting by numbers, such a chore.
You are real and deserve to be sure,
calling you out of blackened rooms.
This love of mine can exhume
the exhausts of your nature.
The way you search for answers
colouring you in.
The beach has its swim;
fast undercurrents drag you.
But you fly as I am with you.
Painted stars are fierce and bright.
See their colours best at night.
But you—my friend, son, maker—
I shall never forsake you.
The fringes of society laugh,
not knowing the task set by me
as your feet find comfort
discovering your masculine way,
covering you in every way.

Coloured

This sublime fantasy I find myself in
brings me your comforts and dwells within me,
calling me to the plunderous untamed sea,
where the seats are comfy and heavens open—
open to all sorts of wonderful creations.
National terror released from bondage to fear.
Come near to me, and I shall give a great start,
fast paced and little knowledge.
The one I bring my solace to, hungry hearts,
thirsty, and needing food.
Brewed in the same pot of joy
where we see our talents deploy.

Where are you going? Who are you?
Speak to me in a beautiful language.
Forage for my words.
Bring me all your beauty.
Tussle with the enemy, and give me what is mine—
you.
Your face amongst many shines forth.
Stars strike me as odd,
the way they move but remain in the universe,
searching for a place to stay
but at home in the sky,
colouring and nurturing our skin.
But be careful.

The nations are calling for comfort.
It is what we are used to and need.
Seeds coming through the soil,
bursting into life with the right food.
Feed us, Lord, with your love.
I need not ask, but is it your need to hear us
fearing not your reply?
Wonderful Lord, take me to the sky,
where colours are intense.
Set up my tent to cover my servants.
Complimentary are your sweet words;
They embed themselves into my soul.
My sound I share with you.
The radio knows this is true.
Serving your country,
slicing the enemy in two.

Furthermore, I have to say
what a wonderful way we seek
our payment to keep us fed,
watered in your sight the fresh relish.
Homeward bound and tested valour,
mighty being strong to win their freedom.
There for the taking, the windows light up.
Today we eat and sup with our friends,
coloured in vogue, making perfect sense.

Colourless

I count it a great blessing,
coming to you, unending joy—
colourless, untainted, and pure.
Mind so clear, I secure
the rights I surely have now.
Somehow, I turn to you and say,
'What a lovely way to be.
Even the dark is as light to thee,
and for me I see your plea
to nurture those who have me.
So darling, my sweet love,
Courting you is my choice,'
as my voice moves alarmingly,
finishing my sentence.
Now I am free, my choice to live
with and for my lady.
Colourless and meekly dim,
this light in you never fades.
You just think it does.
My work is not complete in you.
Sweetness and endurance,
you balance the two.

Kindly see this one through.

Confide in Me

Sensing your desire to see me
as you are would please me,
coming together of our hearts.
Never depart from me
as I go and prepare your way.
Paths I lay for you today.
Kindly ride those waves.
Found in me, your dreams come true.
As important to me as they are,
your safety is my concern.
Walking this earth hand in hand,
pawing over this land of mine,
I catch your breath, and you sign.
Sights of your growth give me life,
bright and shining on that pitch.
Roads you walk come straight to me,
caressing carefully your wife,
certain to combine a real way.
I see it all when you play.
cast astray your former ways.
You have won the day.
Thanks for our praying ways.
No more frays or pulling.
You are my pudding to enjoy,
unemployed and happy.

Country Mile

Missiles do fly day and night.
But your insight overpowers, thus
rendering peace to the city
that ceases to exist.
Missed by the distance
of a current kiss,
dismissed by the tutor
who had enough of the fight.
Draw me peacefully as we change
birds in a cage, but free
this bird of joy: Who is he
that lands on my blossom tree,
caged by its own merit?
Carry it to the mind doctor
who deems it fit to carry on.
So off it goes to my blossom tree,
no cares or worries.
Miles of country to explore,
but my tree she does adore.
Eat of this tree, the provider.
Its dreams are ours as we taste.
Bringer of love to exist
right in the centre of the heart.
Please do not depart from my tree
because my heart could not take it.

Course of Action

I see you, wherever you are.
You cannot escape me and my word.
Shoulder to shoulder, we stand
together in this tiresome land.
Hand in hand, we call our safety.
Land of lands, see a wilting place,
enough to disarm, erasing the chase,
coming into your presence.

In my head I remember your smiles,
stylish actions, and laughing joy.
My boy, you are and you shall stay
beyond all reasoning to show me
your everlasting bond,
dedication not simulation.
Courting my love like a dissertation,
Humbly accepting your plans.
Leave it with me to define you
in a merry sort of way,
praying to you, my bread; my wine
coming in reds, pinks, and whites.

Frightfully drunk was I.
My course changed, and actions as well.

Coursing through My Veins

Capturing my blood-bought freedom,
I see the light in your eyes.
There is no disguise in you.
Parting the waves just for us
because that is who you are.
Through me you part my waves
as I go beyond the sea.
Personally, be kind to my thoughts.
I rattle them out at a steady pace.
Now you know you win over sin.
Through me you have your safety
as you come into my room.
You come in twos as I have made
you to be as one as proposed.
The very scent of you soothes me,
and your conversations are lovely.
I feel me when you call.
We are certain to know it all
as you grow in wisdom and love,
gifts for you from above.
We turn this union into blessings
for the world, that is your ministry.

I am in and with you always.

Courting the Sparrow

You watch me as I sing into the night.
I am a night bird, but I like the day as well.
I swell as I send you these melodies
in this tree I call my home,
devouring my daily feast.
Berries excite me no longer
as I wonder of new ways.

Carry my burdens so I can fly.
Worries weigh me down, so I need a fast supply.
Sensing a dangerous foe nearby,
coursing through my little heart—
little but big.
Swigging my last drink, I dive.
Flapping, I sense a distant call.
My friend Paul has the answers.
Planting my fill as I enjoy it still.
Craftily, I eat in silence and on my own.

Courting the sparrow, my narrow choice.
You are but elegant, free-flowing.
Knowing your destination and comfortable with it,
we sit and think of all we can do.
Fly, you say, so I set my alarm to off.
Do not be alarmed today as you go into it.
These rides are like the wind,
ducking and diving, bringing joy.

It is a freedom we enjoy, and it is all for you.
Trust in the Lord, and he will pull you through.
The freedom you taste is real.
So carry on up the hill, but do not stay still.
Because in life, love, and our seclusion,
learning much as a youth, my son.

Courtyard

Sentenced to a bloody death,
alarmed at your mistreatment,
you felt it was at the end of you.
Chewing and showing your virtue
to fight in the sight of many,
gently you took the torture.
My precious Jesus. I say thanks.
Humility and justifiably raised
praise and glory belong to you.
The passing comments passed on,
you comment on who we belong to.
Your courtyard I cannot imagine.
I know it is great; let me taste
what you wish to give us.
Immersed in heavenly ways,
your heart you make us,
touching our days—your days—
erasing all wrong and doubt.
I cannot count your very accounts
of us in the shade you raised us.
For us you gave it all,
every last drop.
Thanks for everlasting life.
In your presence we are justified,
deemed clean and holy in your sight.
Brightens up my days and moments.
Sweet and lovely you are to us.
Breathe on us your holy musk.

Crossed Legs

They egged me on as I travelled for my supply.
My, oh what a wonderful surprise.
I lay on my back, expecting an attack,
but my Lord, I know no lack.
You hacked at my inability to speak.
Clearly you seek my growth
as I go on unknown until now.
The pastor's house gave me some pleasure
as I was measured by them and found wanting.
But my Father, you are impressed with my best,
very well versed and dressed to suggest
a passing feast as you release these words.
From my lips they pour, but you are my fountain,
One I store from as you supply my lack,
always tracking my mail.

With legs crossed, you emboss my claims
that these words are yours
and not a framework of man's efforts.
Deserted deserts that bring out dry knowledge.
Foraging through these harsh landscapes,
there you are as we escape the burden of waiting
for a food we do not hesitate to enjoy.
Come home, my boy, and look at these plans;
those I have for you, please understand.

It may take a while, but you still smile

through all the world's struggles and dangers.
You run through my arteries as I get up and walk,
stalking my days as we always try to talk.
Look out your window, and find your way.
It is day out there, but mind your steps
as inept creatures try to steal your joy,
inclined to seek another broken toy.
Bleak is the wind that controls our state.

Cute as a Button

Stuttering as you say those words,
I call you, but you are not heard.
Absurd how we come to see
our meal freely enjoyed.
What a girl, what a boy,
calming my nerves as I say, 'Hi,
thanks for noticing me.'
Now I will ask why?
Why, why, oh why do I try
to catch your attention?
When, oh when will I see
your very curvatures?
Can I be your lover's touch?
I dream of you as I climb
the gates I see through.
You see me, but do not open.
Let me in, so I can show
you how a couple can truly grow.
And so I say these wanting words,
'Come home with me,
and be my girl away from the world.
Where you don't cry all your tears
or laugh all your laughs.'

Your task is at hand and clear:
Make me happy, my dear, wonder girl.

Daylight Comes

Where can I see you when you are not there?
How can we dine when you are inclined
the bill to decline and leave elsewhere.
Torn are your days morning, noon, and night.
You politely come out of love and respect.
Come kindly, sir, as I wash out my reasoning.
Condition rubbed in as I keep from sin.
You are the colours that surround me.
You are the flowery incense that carouses me.
Joined in with the hopes of vast comfort,
comfort reaching the whole land.
You feed us all—good, bad, and small—
nurturing our days and dreamy nights.
To settle for the best
in what seems my very undressed moments.
Oh, cumbersome weight you carried.
I carry a little and take up my cross.
Each and every day we blend and toss.
Into the ocean we go as the fish direct me,
mammals and every type of seed.
Free me from my silver tongue
as I breathe within my importance,
casted too close to the ordnance,
frolicking around with my friends on shore.
Animals adore my sense of purpose,
turning into their own surfacing faces,
racing my rescue as I go out into the sea.

Please, sir, can I help?

She wastes little time immediately poised.
The currents pulling this, sure is a tussle.
I care for you, Tim, with every muscle.
You dress in clean attire.
Your soft words are like fire,
spreading and ready for desire to share.
Gospels come in many shapes and forms.
Shalom, my love, I was born to adore thee.
Freely I say how pleasant are your ways.
Follow my lead; you will not stray, ever
tethered to my hip.
I bore you not to flip or trip.
Born again in such a way.
Calm your nerves as I come in love and peace,
respectfully abiding my very word.
Nothing left in me to strive for.
You course through my veins.
You shall never be the same.
Just be tame and don't strain; the rain of blessings is here.
My tears for you are tears of joy.
As you bring these words to the world,
careful as you bring up this girl.

Design

My prized possession.
I see your ascension,
riding high on the clouds.
So what now?

Surfacing from deep,
my witty bit of love to keep
seeping through the unholy cracks.
Stacks of possibilities and probabilities
squeezing my very vein.
My heart reigns in you once again,
once and for all.

Tall and comfortable
in my own skin,
you have won the race.
You are irreplaceable in my eyes.
Winning the prize, you are disguised
as some ordinary folk,
but you are not, by any means, ordinary.
Bordering on genius.
My life courting ladies is for one lady
as I suggest she loves you best.
The others go and lay and dance
until the next one comes by,
ready to go for a ride.

Supplying your every need
makes me bleed my last.
Every seed you have planted,
I will grow up strong.
You belong with me.
You are my own design,
Beautiful in my sight.
I gaze upon you with every right
to share my name in polite prose.
Rising upon those frozen hills,
I jump onto the highest mountain
to reach you there.

Device

Crusty is the ground I sleep on,
made of musty, coarse boxes.
Your blanket is somehow clean.
Your shoes are new.
As we politely chew on the past,
harassed and bullied,
looking for a kick of ego,
turn up your nose to them
for they have today,
but what of tomorrow?
Growing in wisdom and understanding,
your wit so sharp it cuts.
And down they went with a heavy fall.
Their parents taught them nothing,
so it is up to me to teach.
Listening as my heart is glistening,
whispering to each other,
'This guy has guts.'
I see their fall, so I try to stall
naked ambition to pull others down.
My courageous spirit
showed them as clowns
as they frowned on his message:
You may have today,
but what of tomorrow?
It is your choice to receive Jesus.
Your future could be rosy.

So rise to be the one who sent me.

Feeding on Me

Your words see my safety
alive and new daily.
You were never crazy.
Mind a little hazy as we go on.
Pressures from the fight all gone.
You are in reach.
You are my handyman,
understanding the ropes to be pulled.
We are so close right now.
I wish you could stay always.
Life goes on, the waves roll in,
our loves' hearts are always washing in.
The tide collides with every enemy
because this land, my land,
is worth protecting.
We all go on with little mention
of the dissention among the foes.
But we are together, one body,
but oddly apart in the world.
Brought together at church,
lurching onwards, homewards.
Toil of days is over.
Peace and love to both of you,
screwed on tight,
brightens up my day and night.
Politely grasping the situation,
love is always at attention.

Flat or Round

Of course, I came around to the idea.
My love began to settle my debt.
Took my hand, and let her out, her net inept.
Seeing you for the first time, my dearest,
not akin to my loving, wind-feared looks,
sun-shaping waves to form correction.
Can my sharpened tools face my ejection?
So close, you chose my hearty days so clear.

Come, I have prepared a place for you
overfilled with joy with my loving voice.
Do see this one through, my dearest friend.
Your fruits are no cost at all for you.
Come to me with hope, and I shall give you choice.
It is all for you; I shall see your commendation.

Flatten Me

As wide as the story goes,
my to's and fro's count a near miss,
gently displacing misty, foggy lines.
Earthly wisdom we leave behind
as I grind my existence into salt.
Salty and the taste I cannot foretell
until the label reads best before date.
Elated and happy are your blessed hopes.
Utopia awaits my discovery
to form a new kind of release.
Please be with me as I fall to my knees
to worship you at your feet,
total release and thanks in my heart.
My saviour is real and shall not depart.
Of course, I see your tender ways
as we praise you on high,
waiting for your return,
escaping the burning fire made for the wicked,
the unrepentant, and denying my Jesus.
As we wait to be in your arms, Lord,
we wait for the enemy to dissolve.
Problem solved, and now we take our share
of the glorious riches that lead us home,
into your arms, keeping us well,
pure, holy, faithful, and true.
You rescue us when we haven't a clue.
Virtuous and real, I feel your want.

Seal my days with a realistic goal.
In your heart it is all realistic.
As we call your name above all names,
sanely preparing your meal with us,
while we count losses in our lives,
we require to dine in your place.

Flight

This mighty army of ours,
correct in every sight,
carry the cross was your fight,
to show you my heartfelt right.
Politely and softly you came,
taking the blame
for our mistakes.
Your food you share with us
beyond what we understand.
Its taste is sweet and weighty.
You give us plenty for the flight
as we ascend into the night.
We come back full of light.
Figures taste my very calling,
tall in stature and enthralled.
This flight I shall not miss.
Twisting and bending,
the engine rough.
But to my taste, surely enough
we touch base, thankfully safe.
What a flight we made!
Powering through the next one,
hopefully closer to the Son,
carefully and respectfully yours.

Found Your Way

Equipped with my pay, I live to love another day.
Seated at the right hand of God is he.
The course I take where the destination was no mistake.
Taking on the system, my mission is simple,
understanding why the short work as I get paid handsomely.
What are the chances of that?

I keep it all under my hat.

Take up your mat and walk, stalking this man named Jesus,
recklessly opposed to the force.
I wonder what it was all for—
the dangers and loss of life, shattered beliefs.
Certain to retrieve my hopes, however surreal.
Battle won as I eat my three-course meal.
Sealed in victory, I wonder, *What is next?*
Dressed to impress, we come to you wrecked inside.
I wonder why this happened.
You look great, but what separates us?
It is the grimy business of war and loss.
Cost almost too much to bear.
As I take you there under the coverage of my wings,
we still sing as we show how to run.
It is in this direction where you find freedom.
A single bullet shatters the lifetime of builds.
The life we lead is fast but seems so slow.
Encased in a prism as we go on in the beautiful light,

the mighty, my Father, are your delights.
Time is precious; ask for more rights.
Free as a kite dancing in the wind.

Friendship True to the Ear

The courses are evidently useful,
or evidently useless and vain.
But our causes are for the good and just
and not to be swallowed by some wrong choices.
Hear our voices as we choose to declare
we are on the winning team, as each member
is his and in the kiss of love and life.
Coming to a point where it's not essential to survive,
on a knife edge we escape the chop,
correctly driven and an aid to stop evil.
This sequel of the returning king,
guiding and showing us who are our faithful friends.
To the end of the earth, we carry on,
not just the burden of failure, but the success of love.
Turning to my Lord, I ask of your love and wisdom.
I write this in adoration of you, my friend,
supplying me with an acute sense of well-being,
calmly nesting us in the tree of forgiveness,
where with truth we are totally blessed.

Game

Are you game for a sip of sanity?
Are you ready to plant those seeds for me?
As I grow you and yours, I pause for a second.
Then I wonder, *What is the point of living?*

Seeing you for the first time, I pocket your success.
Your honorary means to go on although despondent.
Carry my thoughts to a place of dreams,
where you are protected from all attacks.
What you lack, I want you to come back.
Chase that thought, and put it in its place.
We search to erase all time-killing methods.
Mettle and gumpf can push us so far.
But my Jesus takes us through the tar and mud,
cleans us up, and makes us new,
giving new and precious understanding and wisdom
that only meets in the middle.

Grainy Sand

Washing over Dover beach,
this jellyfish lies in wait,
enjoying playing in the sea.
This enemy had stung me
to the point I had to leave
the grainy, salty sands
that became part of the landscape.
But why produce this enemy?
Out of the shade it swims unaided.
What on earth is that?
Pained and suffering
not the only choices
as this being decides to run,
swimming away from the law.
What jail do they have?
Is it their way or just evil?
Bring me to the till,
and I will fill it with lead.
My protector leads my recovery.
Eventually I breathe relief.
Un-chattering teeth, now I see
the love my Father has for me.
Cover me in protection.

My back is covered as I go forward

Holding Your Hand

I am with you, every challenge you see,
as I come to my impendence, remembrances, and delight,
coursing my way through the wavy days.
Restful nerves come out to play,
my body and mind, I mean every word.
Hearing what was meant to be heard
as I tame your mind and blur your turmoil,
my happy friend, filling your pockets with soil.
The food comes out fresh and delivered.
Received and thanks given to my servant.
Driven into a taste of bliss,
heavenly manna, something I could not resist.
I have raised you to follow me.
I hold your hands as we go our way,
driven in a sense of course of events.
Brilliant how you make ends meet,
Even the poor you regard as rich.

Honest Man

Sincerity of my mind validated,
for further use incorporated.
Majestic are your ways, fighting for a free world
where no one can ring the bell except my son,
and where you seek my every thought.
Your presence is richly looked for.
You can chase me through the muddy paths;
you can see me with your crane like a giraffe.
But we are not seen unless you release our hearts.
You can run, but I will not grow weary.
Tasting, my finding you a victory as I sit and wait.
Plates are full of salted and peppered food.
You have gotten me in a relaxed mood,
where we chew on our words, the terms you use
an honest man shall not be overruled.
As I curl up and eat what was meant for my delight,
no need to wait and given as a surprise,

House on the Hill

Hands in the air will follow my prayer,
undeterred by this ransom served.
Songbirds sing in the heavy morning.
This dawning moment fills me with gladness.
Such a fragment of a man's life
taught me to take a wife full of wisdom.
History teaches me that when one door closes,
another one opens—or maybe three or four.
Hitting the floor with a bounce,
protecting my mind, every ounce,
accounting for the richness I have been given.
No house or car but experience and achievement,
bereaved by the changing pace of the world.
This planet is in hunger for rest.
Suggest a way that should portray solidarity.
The house on the hill forgot time.
Symphonies mention why the time changes.
Pages and pages follow the line.
'Get in line', they say, but I wanted to get out.
Give me a shout about the times changing,
waging war against terror.
Remember how it all started, you and I.
Nice as pie as I try to bring us together.
Treat me as a wonderful royal kin.
Bin the enemy to bite the dust,
trusting in a touching way.

Our Father and friend at the weekend
breathes life into us before the touchless figures,
giving us vigour, cementing our love.
Above riches of this dark world
there you are, being beams of light,
a mighty stance against the underworld
that tries to stop us as we hurl
position against fruition.
You are my fresh, sweet fruit to eat;
what a tasty treat you are.
Fast and fair, the hairs on your head are numbered,
knowing every one of our thoughts.

I Adore You

I know your flaws, but I shall not ignore them.
Your sights and wise insights I shall improve.
Moving away with nothing to choose
would have been a big mistake
as I am with you every moment, awake or asleep.
Even in a hazy daze I can get to you.
Your love for me shall shine.

On the ward you play your part,
hearty laughs and a studious heart,
where you do not know it all.
Tall in stature and in grace.
I shall not erase your achievements.
Deleting them would be a crime
because your thoughts are mine, sunshine,
keeping me informed at times.
Making wise choices, you grace the sky,
like a tall skyscraper but higher.
Politely, I call you out.
The clouds are soft-spoken, but I am softer.
I am wanting to see your delightful face
praising me as you go on.
I struggle to keep up, Lord,
but I shall win this for you.
Crying out to the sky, 'What a lovely view!'
True to me you stay and always.
Our paths meet on the road to my place,

tasting the best there is to be,
I search your heart; I find it beautifully kept.
Into keeping
where I carry you to every meeting,
undermined but unafraid, no illusion believed,
and your soul is with me.

I Am Using You

You may not always know when or why
the end to your suffering is nigh.
I believe you to be a little shy.
Care for a tea with me, and you shall see
where you are and where you want to be,
courtesy of your maker and best friend.
My love for you, not just for the weekend,
blending and mingling, singing and believing,
seeking and searching, both blinding and knowing.
I remember you at your school.
That one wasn't meant for you, but you still grew
into a man who shall know my plans for him.
Sentries protect and rise,
but you, my friend, are in disguise.
Not for long and witness their demise.
And look them right in their eyes and say,
'I know my Father, and he knows me.
I will pray for you and make you see
how beautiful I really am.'
When you were at sea, I saw a making of you
made to fight and slaughter.
Who wears the victor's crown? It is I.
All beginnings, some cumbersome and slow,
yours is fast, and you are in the know.
Growth outnumbering your piers.
I come to your rescue; I have done for years,
roping off the dangers and snares.

What an experience just to see you shine!
Thank you, Father, all is fine and dandy.
I pray for your cause, not a shanty town.
I kneel before you as I sit and know,
my Father, you know I don't need a spectacle
or public showing and gaining respect.
It is easy to see you in your way.
Every day I show, but sadly, some walk away,
burdened with doubt; but oh, such a happy day
and far away from danger,
I remember the manger.

I Bled

Searching the path, not being misled,
you taught me to see and be what you want me
to be; I look down to avoid the cracks.
And I look back to see if you are watching.
I trip, but not far, as I stumble through life.
Found myself a wife who cares for my needs.
Bless her, Lord, and her wonderful world
as this girl of mine comforts me.
We dine in the best restaurants,
not counting the cost anymore
as we store our memories for the future.
We nurture our growth, and you pine for us both.

You bled that we may have life and have it to the full.
But the raging bull tries to derail us and our plans
as we go on together hand in hand.
We course through this land, and no danger found.
Living this life is like a pound of bananas.
Bizarrely enough, you still want to talk with us.
What a Father, what a God, what a leader.
Always wanting to please you as we go on.
This song of yours in waiting,
never debating its quality or sanity.
A hand full of pity led me to change
as the rage of the storm was willing to destroy.

I bled and nearly died.

My Lord, you watch me as I try
asking for a contrite and pure heart.

I See You

In the corner,
I know you are shy.
But don't cry; I am here to help.
In uncertain forms I dwell in you.
Take me to the surface,
where the blessed stars face me.
I don't want your indifference.
I don't want your crying shame.
I want your story to watch and be.
Searching you carefully,
we spread the cost.
Seeing you in the corner,
remembering your childhood,
I wonder if I should
name and crosses.
Costly to me, you are.
I will never let you go.
Pausing to think, but not too much.
Sinking into your comfy chair,
you stare at creation,
feeling for it as I do,
not plumbing down to the deep.

Keep in me as I weep for it.

In the Desert

Taking the right turn, I mourn for you
as I search your corner.
Brought out of trouble and despair,
close by, in my heart, I feel you there
in the deserted town, abandoned in time.
Perfectly raised my abased charm
to be desired and wanted.
You certainly have a lot,
and you flaunt it on the spot.
My desert, where people drop,
I wish you the best as we go on.
Something will turn up, surely,
levering my body to carry on.
The Son is my only escape.
We play, believing we shall be safe.
Naval bases far from the action.
Flight is the only way,
keeping our eyes open to send a flare.
Come up, I want to be there for you.
Truly feeling somewhat bemused,
carrying on across the border
between nations so very different.
Segments of humanity, hear my plea.
Now I am in England, we will surely be
protected and cared for,
education, healthcare, and settlement.
I totally understand

you are healthy and happy,
taking your burden so far away.
So far it is not in existence.
Maybe you can pray for my health.
My girl next to me,
what else is in store for us
wandering this land, deserted.
We, your fans, are worthy of you
through your Son, Jesus Christ,
rising above the ashes of a desolate world,
seeing your works are close at hand.
Planned are your goals for us to expand
courtesy.

Land of Plenty

Sentry duty once again, sparking a feud.
My friend, where are your rights?
Tighten up your belt and end the supply.
We are in a land of plenty.
Carefully silenced by allotted wars,
sorted into baskets concerned for the youth.
Truth prevails once again,
beginning a mighty stance of solidarity.
Home-born abilities stretch my facility.
A place of experimentation,
this land of plenty extends to you,
brought me your wish and your breath.
Gifts for now and tomorrow,
cast away the junk and sorrow,
burrowing to borrow another cent.
Bent on defeat are your enemies
as we cast them down into prison.

Alas, we arrive on to a plucky ride,
not too fast and not too scary.
Many get off early, but you stay
until the end, where your strength supplies
knightly days and surfacing nights.
Politely calling family to extend
a loving voice; the weekend is near.
Choices brought me here to this place.

Still alive and saved by grace,
capturing my meal and searching still
for something better.

Scatter the foes entrenched in woes.
These horror plots will not grow;
They shall not take over me.
As true as you are, you are my safety,
portraying my very life and soul
that the world needs to see.
Combining the work you have for me,
freely given and freely enjoyed.
Employed and *deployed* are your words.
Sentiments and elegance can be he.
Your joy follows me everywhere.

Lily of the Valley

Wandering your freshly made fields,
you see my voice as it grows.
Triumphant entry, yes, they know
how to dress to impress
this lily of the valley.
One can try to describe
in a way that flaunts his colours
even into the nightly gain.
I sense your framed picture,
one of beauty and innocence.
Come, and I shall show you life,
a life of giving and seeing,
believing you are beautiful
even as they cut you
and display in your homes,
modestly coloured as they shrink.
Bring me back to the fields,
where I am meant to be
seeking my home amongst the fields.
The rain touches me as I feel you,
the wind plays with my hair,
and passersby stare at us
as we thrust out our lives.

Memories

Plenty around, but all I see
is personal favour of the others
growing out of trouble.
Where is mine? I begin to think,
your personal wonder in the drink.
I search my mind, but all I feel
is the reeling cough of mine,
wanting it to subside outside,
colliding through written faults,
plans we have not felt in a sense.
I know this life has more.
'Away with the pretence,' I say.
Let us make and live memories
as we go through our day,
praying and asking, 'Where are you?'
as I look in the bins for rescue.
My cast-iron will and strength
mean nothing as I talk at length.

Memories, precious memories cease,
bilingual in my sight
easing my polite cause,
bring me my gauze to sift my food.
Memories that brewed are for me
as I pass on through this channel
of a life led by will.
Better for us and better my thrill.

Mistakes Forgiven

We come in small packages, taught to wait.
Displacing a colourful Father, I wait.
Trying his best to erase the past,
but I come with honourable intentions.
Mention me as a call out to you,
a formidable force just like you
through these strange and somewhat confusing times.
Blinded by those travelling eyes,
surfacing even through those dark skies.
Matching you and hatching a plan of safe dwellings,
fortified ruins, and mannequins dressed for it.
The wars that cause so much distaste and destruction.
Heavenward we look as the burden is lifted.
Of course, there are trials and misfit clothes.
Roaming and controlling foes, a heavy dose.
Fortune tells me we need no fight
because my Father is here to save the day.
Sons of peace, carry us straightaway from wars.
No more battles and no more divorce,
sharpened like a tenuous tool.
Where is my drinking stool; close by, I assume.
Those ruined relationships are nudes to me,
undressed and without covers.
Another sentence becomes another.

Forgive and relive our pasts? We forgive to relive
all the workmanship you aspire to provoke
a work in progress in me, I am sure.
Colours in your heart still shine forth
during these lessons we learn in life.
Bringer of lived dreams, please understand.
With me, you played a true and straight hand,
forgiven and bringer of life.

My Lord and Saviour, bring them out of their ruin,
and choose the right path to serve you,
virtuous in accentuals and accentuates me.
Always a home to come to at the end of the day.
Never hungry, and you made my living quarters fresh,
painted, and laboured for my hazy mess to be a dad.
But all I want is your loving approval.

Moods

Fruitful amongst many,
casting your bait amongst many,
she don't bite who feeds.
Cooking for you,
spreading your seeds afar,
never married but belonging
to my heavenly Father, my all.
In the grand scheme of things,
we seem so small in comparison,
but we are big in his heart.
Laughter and joy, a gift for us.
We tend to them well as we wash.
Our insides are clean and pure,
ready to receive what is for you.
Breathing and making amends
to our former selves
that were left on the shelves.
Healthy, we show a glow.
We know what many do not—
that our story has a great plot.
Moods and trance enter my thoughts.
For a while, we look finished,
But there is so much to do.
Fading into my very existence,
I come with perseverance.

Muscle

Keeping it pumping, heart not to depart.
Feeling stumped? Ask the Father,
who gives freely all good things,
the giver and bringer of light.
My body may be waning and tight.
Your body keeps me with insight.
Muscle me in to these wonderful blessings.
Dressed to impress, are you making impressions?
Mention my body and all its delights.
My plights loosened as we see in the night,
correctly poised to make an alarming discovery.
These calls used to frighten me
but not anymore.
At the core of my innermost being,
my heart wants to retreat but stays close.
My vigour I doubt as I lose my foes,
shoes with toes poking out of their walls.
Call me as I suggest a cure for menopause.
Struggling to see the reality of it all.
Lord, I come to you to show you
I am here, waiting on your call.
Felt a trip but not falling.
Trials and painful exploits.
Chosen muscles do flex in time.
Chiming like chimers that come along
to share your vote and claim me strong.
We belong with you, Lord.

I take the sword and slay your haters.
They use us as wine tasters,
never putting their lives on the line.
See me, and I shall touch your life,
kindly coming into this wonder of yours,
pausing for thought and pawing our way
through the very dust that lays.
A dusty blanket over seekers of the light
attempts to blind us from the truth.
I take down my enemy in one swoop.
Gone is he and shall never return.

We turn to each other and say,
'Well done', for we have won the day.

My Child

I come to you in peace.
Your ageing has ceased,
breathing as you search
beneath the earth for life.
No need to search any longer.
Lingering hopes grow stronger
as I ponder on your life.
My child, my beautiful child,
cast your cares on me.
Tell me your stories.
Am I in them?
Tell me your fears.
Are you scared?
I am not afraid of who you are.
We can fly.
Rich is the man who invests
in me.
Deeds done for the cause
brought me your pleas.
As we search your answers
for your wisdom, precious wisdom
that surpasses understanding,
fling me your rope.
I shall keep you close,
safe in the knowledge,
safe in my Holy Ghost.

My Daily Meal

Sealed with approval, I dance this way.
With careful planning, you save our day.
Going on in haste, wasting opportunities,
the lady reveals her hand.
Branded a cheat for all her master plans,
revealing her secret as to say,
'Lord, I asked for it this way.'
My daily meal nourishing and satisfying.
Not lying when I say that it is good.
But our special meals, every single one,
having fun indoors to tickle the senses.
Applause to my very nature of wettened wit,
taking the family to see the sea.
Fish and chips by the sea, what a delight!
Politely I get the notion to leave,
but the ocean calls me back to retrieve my story.
Elegantly she washes my feet,
never wishing defeat on my kin.
This water roars, and I jump straight in,
pinning me to the floor.
I am exploded into the sky,
way above the waves; as I push with all my might,
politely, the waves wish a goodbye.
Crying, I sense annual leave.
Believe me when my spirit wishes you well.
Tell me of your days dwelling in secret.
I want to know what keeps you going.

Sewing? Drawing? It is all fun.
But what of your polarity? What of your son?
Casting away from troubles and strife,
a kindled spirit is me and my wife.
Create in me a spirit of yearning,
yearning for you and your truths,
that eradicates all worldly wisdom.
Come soon, and remove me from this prison.
Talking in unison, my fruition I give you.
Parting the ways that restrict us from us,
talking of a place where righteousness is key,
locks broken to set us free.

My Delivery

Searching for your smile,
I realised it's a delivery.
Delving into your heart of hearts,
you show me my centrepiece
of defining humanity,
deferring from calamity,
sent for me my duty,
my marital duty,
outfoxing my adversaries
as my Father put in me
to search my heart for reality.
Treasure me as I do you.
These caring tender hands
rescue more than a few
from torrid notions of wealth and war
because it is not what
we are fighting for.
Shaken to the core, you bore me.
Wondrous free tendencies.
Tend to my branches and leaves.
Fruits of your taste so sweet.
Please don't hold them from us.
Fighting the dusty terrain
makes the body's frame shake.
Waking to see another day of this;
I surely would not want to wake
to a case of mistaken identity.

My Diamond

I found you under rubble,
where trouble was your daily meal,
suffered under pretence and order.
Seeing you suffering, I bring you
to the surfacing arrangement,
tasking you to redemption,
where there is no dissention.
Mention me when you go home.
I have a lot to give you.
Coursing through my body,
a yearning to help and serve.
You have found in me strength
to be found and cleaned,
cut like a special rock that shines,
pining for your success and reality—
but a reality that brings joy.
Eternally with me are your choices,
every day hearing voices of comfort.
I shall never desert your heart
or part ways with you near.
We are certain to bring home
another family member.
Remembering your clamour for a place,
facing your foes with grace,
pacing out of trace,
and facing my fears and hard years.

My Distant Hopes

When I called you, you were there.
When I trip or fall, you are there.
When I cry my sorrow into the night,
you are there.

When I find my peace, it is from you.
When I feel the soft sun on my face,
you are watching, waiting for my smile.

When I played as a child, you watched.
Now when I write, it is you.
When I climb, you make sure I am safe.
When in hospital, you are my nurse.
When I run, I am always first.

This thing called life,
chiding and pulling us through you do,
chopping the wood we could never build with,
making sure we are not landfill.
Until we are, you carry us through.
In my mind, I sense your pleasure,
watching us as we treasure your Word.
These hearts you give us to protect,
but in reality, they are in your keeping,
seeing what you do with it
and whom you share it with,
lifting abilities to carry and hold.

It's all your space, Lord, to fill.
We are wide open to receive your will.
For our lives, we wonder still.

The pleasure is mine, my friend.
As we casually bend and kneel
for you, my Lord, I feel my life slipping
away from decay, stripped of all force.
It is hereditary that you steady me
for I am on sentry duty.

My Frog-Eyed Sprite

Furthermore, to my frog eye,
it was a sprint to the finish.
Over age, your charm does not diminish.
Flirting with my earthly wishes,
I turn to you with the ones I am sure of.
My sprite, enhancing the ride,
customs aside, I shall change your colour.
Bucket seats and straps to match.
Your hubs could wrangle up the cash.
My frog-eyed sprite, made for fun,
the elite would pass it off.
But to me, you are my medal of honour
as we ride as smooth as a slide.
Your capacity is low, suspension wobbly,
but you sure do go around the bedside table.
Created you to arrive in style,
you caught my attention right away,
rusting and pulling to the left.
Otherwise, you were left in decay.
And then he purchased you with blood.
Whom else would pay in this way?
Only the one who celebrates our days,
moments of praise, and courage to state,
'I love you, my dear, and do not fear.
The stakes are high, but I am always there,
paring off the demand for more.'
You give enough for my fervent store.

Jesus paid for your bread and wine,
making you shine in the limelight,
delighting in giving us support
to watch us play all these sports
caught off guard my maid of honour.
Next it is you; my sprite has no clue.
Surfacing geraniums and plants of colour
watch me as I uncover discoveries,
freeing me from the surface mildew.
Here I go again on my field trip.
Any excuse for a last ride,
never hiding you from your fans,
the boss, and my handiwork admired.

My Future

Sensing your frameless wonder,
pondering on the sight of sad plunder,
shoulder to shoulder, I come in pale blue.
When the sun is rising in the sky,
it is a wonder why we cry.
We do not know why or how we serve
as our culinary delights deserve.
Virtue is a feeling of space and wisdom,
carrying the burden of an unloved servant
known by many sentries long ago.
I felt somewhat alarmed as time goes too slow.
My inventive taste and the aura of your face
coming to you, I have won the race.
Never erasing our need for haste as you glow
in my presence, and then you will know
why the wind blows so hard
into the unknown distance.

My House and Castle

Masterfully, I write to you, undivided.
Cast your cares on me as I ask of your delights.
Presently, I vow to make all your dreams come true.
Personally, I care to be your everything,
sparkling in the great sunshine.
The moon and all things bright
ghastly fear, and all the years of the unkept,
she wept as I called out your name.
Neither fortune nor fame but a works sent for me.
Brilliantly, you smile into the void,
where your accurate calls chide.
Take these moments for you to come inside,
capturing your smile as I take a look inside
further to your ambition raised.
Our hopes of a better life in this world fade,
but the futures for us in your arms are made.

Courageous spirit, I detail your thoughts
of a hallucinogenic wind which plays the note
that calls me home, my home and castle,
where I ask for little but am given big.
Swigging on this pure juice so lovely,
I jump up to see your heart.
I call your soul to be where I am
in my heart and in my mind.
Kindly you define my state.

Your stature of a tale of lived fate.
Success came at my Saviour's costly blood.
The one we could not pay ourselves,
an offering of the highest order.
Pleasing and beautiful is your Son.
You told the whole world where it all began.
Such a sight to behold, your true beauty.

Your stature of a tale of lived fate.
Success came at my Saviour's costly blood.
The one we could not pay ourselves,
an offering of the highest order.
Pleasing and beautiful is your Son.
You told the whole world where it all began.
Such a sight to behold, your true beauty.

My Imaginary Rabbit

I can see your clothed body.
Somebody should look out for you.
I see you in my dreams as I burst happily
out of my hutch and into the garden,
spared a punishment for eating your carrot,
a mascot for my erratic footballing needs,
hatching a plan to get some freedom
as I dig to within an inch of my life.
Crumbling and tumbling are your walls
that try to keep us apart.

Your hearty laugh and half-hatched plans
keep me coming back for more air you send.
Let's not present each other for the weekend.
Let's give us Monday back again.

Common mice and rubber balls
keep me waiting for life from the hutch.
My little rabbit, I love you so much.
Here's to you and your escape, my friend.

My Little Treats

You bring me home, into your understanding.
Pounding hearts landing their vehicle
with a wheel missing.
This prison called this body,
worn and trod on and made blind to the world.
Surely my shore leave will not go wrong
as I bring you those pearls, the ones I dug for you,
the ones I searched tirelessly to find
with grimy, cold, deserted hands.
These plans I have for us
could have dissolved in an instant,
but our skin means we are watertight.
Our might and strength come from the one
who showed us right from wrong.
Let us burst into song
where we belong, among the merry throng,
realising we are part of a huge family,
where our voices and choices earnestly give
blessings in our lives and the strength to forgive.
And live among the family tree,
where we are protective and protected.
Your needs never neglected.

So when I talk of little treats,
they are meant to land you right back on your feet.
You get up out of your seat.
We cause you to beat your foe.

You rise, and the undergrowth is detached.
Do the maths, and you shall see.
Mightily you turn to me and ask,
'What happened to you, and why do I ask?'
Classes given to open up our voices.

My Need

Of course, I decide what I want and need,
breeding this seed we both want to grow.
Come here to know my heart.
It's all good to know where to start.
Costly mistakes and debating my ratings,
it's all for us, our future, our place.
Coming together, we shall win this race
as we bleed through these pages,
unable to see what they want from this life.

We are together in our thoughts,
reeling away the tone of the courts.
Sorts and such must believe that we are here
to make a difference in this world.
Believe me when I speak of your future.
For you, I make it a good one.
New day, new hour, new minute, new second—
bearing news, it goes in an instant.
What did you say? I do not remember.
Coming together as we grow,
for you, I seek your joy to be you again.

It is all I need to be your friend,
knowing your future is secure
and that you feel it inside when on a mad ride.
My centred secure truth that I willingly make
all for you; do not throw it away.

Changing my muscles into softness
was definitely a good move as you are deterred,
removed from the fight; I do it for you.
Coming together, let's see this one through.
Choices made into the night carry my sleep.
Modes of sleep and brave sheep nightly weep
as I take this over.
Try to stay sober; it is best for you and us.
Caressing my lines, you do it so well.
Targeting my mail as I sense some on my doorstep.
Weathered hopes are my immediate concept;
drew me in and wept for me.
Thank you.

My Pet Bat

I found you battered in action.
Placing my hand upon your head,
opening your wings, and then I knew
this bat was not meant for the night.
Protecting me and my inside insights,
you see where others can't, a great companion.
Wasting little time, I hid you in my cloak.
I feel you cold and trembling.
Pain that would have nearly killed me,
you brush it off as I sing to you.
You come out in the day.
Those other peers of you could not say what the day holds for you,
but I see your future, and it is shapely.
My best friend, my pet bat,
torn after birth away from the crowd.
Your disability, is it really a hindrance?
Patiently waiting for confidence to grow
between us, oh, what a show.
An all-seeing, all-dancing bat.
I surely could not have planned that.
My knees shake as I leave you home,
but one day he will have his own.
Cast your cares on me; you shall be free.
In all certainty, I realise
you do not need eyes to see.
Displaying you to all my friends,
you cope where others fail to see

this bat is you and a part of me
succeeding in your bidding.
Hidden in the rubble are our golden tickets
to keep hold of until the day I come.
The numbness will go, sensations overflown,
caught in the chase, you are wise in your stance,
romance, and remembrance.

My Plummer

Came at a pace, like running a race.
Before me I feel, kneeling,
my meal, you believe in me.
Sealed with your spirit
everything you are.
Nothing from me you need.
Perfectly you formed my seed,
bringing gifts as we plead for you,
bleeding and broken.
Lord, you are always outspoken.
Mention me as you rise.
Oh, what a wonderful surprise.
We wear no disguise,
and being with you,
you are our endless supply,
supplementing us with your Word,
your supernatural Word,
bringing life, light, wisdom, peace.
You course through me and I in you.
This one is for you
as I come to a surpassing feast.
I come to you needy and diseased.
As you pray over me, I feel senseless.
You ask of my freedom.
Seaborne, I ask for your direction.
I detect an element of reason
that you are the one to follow my dreams.

Harpoons missing their targets,
we escape without harm.
Napalm struck, and many were burned.
Such an awful way to die.
Some lived with the scars.
The battle is yours and not ours.
Breaking into song, my last breath
dawning as we pass over
the death and life of my Jesus,
sent to serve you, begin my journey,
get up silently.
Bright lights sometimes wake the host.
But what I fear most is losing
my Jesus, always at hand to comfort.
Every moment is fresh and new.
I salute you
as I chew through my situation
to make a brighter day a sensation.
Giving and receiving, it's all in choice.
Give and receive, that is your voice.
Search me; make me new.
A few make it, and you are the few
coursing my interest, and I bless you both.
My children you are; what more do I need?

My Search Is Over

To bind and play round this place of mine,
castles and forts come into mind.
Playfully pushing along the road
an all-seeing familiar rock on the hill.
I go up there to find my choice among the voices.
They watch and listen to what I say.
Forming those words in my mouth, I pray to my Father.
Plundered precious moments metallically inscribed,
not denied my prize finishing the race.
Best face forward, I praise my Jesus.
Pleasing us, he does his duty.
Cream of the crop and sensory enhancement,
wards full of missing ambition.
Keep your ammunition for when you need it.
Together we shall rise
amongst terrors casting fear into the night,
where our delights fail just for a moment,
and then it is gone.

My gentle spirit moves on and on,
carnivorous ways feeding on us.
But we still dance into the night.
The morning was so good.
Understanding the flight of our ride,
sliding and weaving, ducking and diving,
the ride of a lifetime,
where we lose track of time.

Crime is finished, and the pain removed.
I take my share and spread the moody food.
I sup when in your company.
Better that way than to gorge and force it down,
mucky fingers your viscosity.
Runs through your hands,
around the fingers,
lingering in italics,
singing into the mic,
recording my visage.
It has been a wonderful ride.
As we sense your human spirit—
particularly as fruit pie—
into your keeping we give our spirit,
kindled and relieved
as we walk on by.
Being young, our earthly desires fade,
laden into the prize of a well-made surprise,
where dreams come real.
I sense that you have come to my door.
Knock, and it shall be opened.
Seek, and you shall find.

My Very Nature

It is natural to think of the ways
we seek our lives to sing it,
singing a joyful song to encounter
someone who presents themselves
in a full body of health.
My very nature describes its fiction.
Home brought gifts from the skies,
fickle in essence but amazingly read.
Every power that you describe
comes straight from inside.
Cries for justice ring true.
Heavenly devotion is given to you,
just like the ways we give gifts,
a good one encountered rarely.
Such as my feelings of deep peace,
unique to my own children.
Passing away, and legacy carries on
throughout the ages to come.
Learning to push forward
to the goal set for reward.
My core of pain removed faintly.
I suggest you go on in your title …

of my saintly friend and believer.

True Lovers Find

Changes and chances
come in an instant.
Mesmerizingly simple,
caught in my daze.
Seen are my leaves,
and seen are my ways.
Hopes for your safety.
Maybe you feel me.
Where are thy thoughts?
They long for you.
Come to my table of dreams.
What seems to be real?
To me, it's what I sense.
That mindfulness comes.
Seek my blessings,
remove my bandages, my dressings.
To me, you are worth it.
Labels put on you, I see the truth.

On My Own

I found a pound of flesh,
fresh residence casting a pest
thrown in a room with nothing,
not even my Father's written Word.
Absurd to see that these days.
Has the plot been lost?

On my own with my thoughts,
caught up in Nordic air systems,
the air conditioning changes,
screaming to let me go.
Another form to fill in, eh?
As they watched me—
their beady eyes watched me—
as I fought my attachment to porn.
Born this way as humans exist
to please themselves in a twist.

This room of mine I can escape
only by spiritual awakening.
If only I could fly, I could find
the way out of the binding ways.
Waves and drifting vessels,
on board are my nets to catch.
Batten up the hatches.
Freedom's egg has been hatched.
By my imagination, I am free.

Call to me; I am always here,
chanting your freedom.

Opening Line

I call you, and you come out to play.
My curtsey for the queen missing
as I stroll through the gates
in less than a whisper as I cross the line
between sane and outlandish.
It is easy for me to deliver the mail.
But carry it? Oh, I could surely faint
as my dainty toes and my makeup smudged.
Still, I go to the palace full of intent
or realise the truth of the coronation,
its ability to fade and ride that wave.
Imagine her on my surfboard,
if I ever did own one.
I assure you 'twas not stolen,
and my alibi is the queen.
Quite a good reliable one I put to the judge.
My opening line could it be said
with a straight face but rarely a straight tie.
Putting on my socks, accidentally matched,
girlish hair, and trendy smile.
I have this one in the bag.
Dragging my heels and stamping my claim,
is there any wonder I need to entertain?
My earth dad taught me nothing apart from fear.
Year after year, in pretence as I say to him,

'I can grunt in my own flat'; he went away miffed.
I am here, creased shirts and trousers,
underwear to despair my comfort zone
as I pull and tug at them down the street,
my not-so-neat hair and depleted rations.
Calm in my own skin, I politely begin to
wear those clothes too high up the cuff,
unearned and not deserved, undeterred by fear.
Now I can clear my throat in peace
and compliment my wife on my tasty treat.
Curtsey shown to my many fans.
I brought you here, now do you understand?

Our Journey

A straight path isn't always the quickest.
Running fingers through my hair, yeah, I'm the slickest.
My girl next to me I call my missus.
For the race, yeah, I'm the fittest.
Each and every pass, I'm at the finish.
Faithfully bound by sound and wishes,
our love and faith will never diminish.

You are my man, and I do understand
that I will meet you in every way I can,
getting to know my family clan.
Together, we shall make our plans,
walking through life hand in hand,
helping others to understand
how lovely Jesus is in the land.

He taught us how to love and give,
shaking and straining us—like a sieve.
Our brothers and sisters, who we forgive,
realising it's a good way to live
our life, and his love is a beautiful gift.

Letting his spirit move within us,
our souls in his keeping we trust.
Praying and searching faith is a must.
The windy, blowy days causing a gust.
Peace within us, no work, no thrust,
taking us home, no kicking, no fuss.

On my mind in my sleepy state,
dreams come together, a clean slate.
Senses fill us to the brim to elate.
we finish our meals, nothing left on the plate.
It's our future, our destiny, our arrival for fate.

In us you dwell; we found our safe place.
Between us there is no time or space.
We found freedom out of life's maze
as upon his wonder we gaze.
Dream states finding, searching for your face,
seeing his beauty in every place.
Yesterday's struggles are all erased.

(Timothy Green and Magdalena Judge)

Our Refuge

Mention us as we try to fly.
I see you as my refuge.
As a refugee, I want to say
my pay gets bigger each and every day
thanks be to my Maker,
my waiter, and Creator.
Simulating the waiting times,
occasionally crossing the line.
I find my fine not earned or gained,
impaled on my work and words.
I will not shake it off
or begin a deterrent of war.
Our war is against principalities
and not with flesh as is said.
At the end of our day together,
we say and give thanks.
Portraying your ways
in this earthly maze, where we carry
upon our shoulders the pain of life.
Life in a sense of loss.
But true blessings of life are not bought.
You cannot earn it, but it is received.
Believing it is yours is a good start.
You rattled some cages; oh, boy, you have heart.
Refuge is your way, depleted until pay.
Lazy days in the sun,
it is the way you are, my son.

No work tiresome for you.
You take it or leave it, believing truth.
Youthful ambitions are achievable.
No deceit found in you.
We carry this one through.
As you are landed by the sea's waves,
bringing you in on a torrid sea,
personally, I shall see to thee.
Your personality is growing and in favour.
No more labouring for you.

Promises

It is kind of sad
when we talk about what we had.
What about what we have?
Shaking and raking up the leaves,
a sorrowful sight when I see them
being blown and carried
to another place in time.
Where is their stability?
It was in the vine
as they whine of their lot,
not required to discover the plot.
Rot removed, and the skin soothed,
not removed from humanity,
groomed and made well.
I promise you now,
take cover and survive;
I shall be with you always.
Though the airwaves are not seen,
it is the best way to bring me
to the masses; radio is still key.
Your learning ways not to be pitied.
Cities on the top of the hill,
come to us; we shall demonstrate
the plan we have for our sake.
Buried beneath the tree,
the one you made just for me.
Carry and marry, she is the one.
Don't let this one go.

Questions Answered

As I depart with this everyday joy,
through me, I see lacking in plot,
not through lack of insight
as once was questioned.
But mention this as I grow:
Your questions are important,
and so are the answers to them.
Soldier hemmed in from all sides.
Isn't it a wonder we try to change
this very world on to the page,
furrowing and burrowing the land.
Canned goods last,
but the words stay fresh in us.
As we think about them,
ten to a dozen, we work and strive.
This wondrous existence
we are trying tonight.
Get up and see your beauty
as in a mirror, yours is real.
Looking on at this surreal image,
pasted before me on my canvas,
where I can change my shape.
No need of tape to rearrange.

Release My Walk

Talking was a foreign affair.
You talk and walk as if you were there,
baring your case of innocent plea.
Where were you when it happened?

Release me as I walk.
Release me as I talk.
Bearing these troubles for you,
it's what I do.
A new and improved you
staring back at me through the wall.
Sentenced but driven,
the dove calls its friend.
Bending at will, you still relent,
journey on tour, and shall soon end.
Be my guide as I tend your crop,
easing me into a core of substance,
enough to sail a cumbersome vessel.
Invest in me, and I shall free you.
I shall bring you to realise
my walk with you not compromised.
Skies are the limit; I make a choice.
Voice your opinion,
one that is backed up by the Bible.
It is a reliable source to life.
Carrying forward to pruning knife,
use it well, sustaining my life.

Slavery

Come to me, all you slaves
bundled into their graves.
Honestly, I come to the age
of free hopes of glory.
My story of tender mercies
often beyond recognition.
My ammunition to defend my home
tussled in fruition.
My statement I wholly enfold
the earth and its riches,
not meant for my taste.
Casting out my shadowy entrails,
where there is blood and haste.
They deface the face of my brothers
as they sip on merrily in their gaze.
We praise our Father,
protecting our soul and spirit,
tasting promises within ourselves.
Clearly, we are taken off the shelves
as this world presses on.
We do not belong here.
This world is not our home,
just a dwelling for our resting.

So Rock and Roll

He sat, he waited, he mused,
looking down at his shoes, thinking.
Her picture made him cry
and got him drinking.
Normally in sobriety, sound of mind,
close to the edge, but who cared?

Getting dressed late afternoon,
wishing sleep would come soon.
Weeping constantly, sodden, and scared,
maimed, bitten, and left to die.
The sky watching, thinking, *Why, oh, why?*

And then …
He went, grabbing his guitar.
Nobody thought he was any good.
A star in the making, dreams revived and waiting.
Shaken by his look, what a poser; he laughed.
Taken a new role, and passers-by sought revival.
His time has come to glue his tattered pages
and write another story.

She smiled, his heart leapt, keeping, and kept
self-styled and assured.
Saw from a mile the sunshine she brought.
What a handsome man, she thought.
By his blood had been bought.

Blood thickened as it flowed.
What happened? No one knows.
Being and feeling and seeing.

Sound the Horn

Foraging for my homebound choice
that will lead me to my home,
voice your outward opinion
where rats are keen and healthy.
The sign roads go pleasantly
into the night, often lacking in sight,
politely calling my centrepiece.
Wars curdle around my knees,
missionaries wasted amongst enemies.
Rightful opinion, rack and pinion,
slightly out of place.

Handwritten providence
scars, sealing that fateful day.
The ones I don't see inscribed
following the noisy parade,
in battle forcibly enslaved,
slain by their own tongues
whence someone suggested a song.
Bring our boys home.
The boys are back in town.
Covered in paint,
made certain to establish himself
as the patron saint of Ukraine,
saving his ever-growing medical cases.
Took a bullet, wasting little time,

the sentry of his post.
Silence can be dangerous
when the attack out of the blue
chews away what peace you had left.
It occurs in the silent night.
This fight is yours, Lord.
Take them with the sword of the spirit.
Send them into place amongst rabble.
And that is what they are—rabble.
Moving targets seen and then felt.
Herds of them coming from the hills.
It is light, and we are ready,
the enemy in swarms of black.
Lord, take me back to sound the horn.
Torn by their making,
formless shadows await their destruction.
A potent mess of lies and illusion
cast out into their own seclusion.
Mention my name and gain favour.
Flavour of victory settled my nerves.
Observe the law.

Stacking the Shelves

I am carrying you to be laid
across the park to a parade,
saying what should be said:
'Strong will and a head of wool,
fluffy and warm, we love you still.'
Strange ways and stranger people,
the odds of carrying you, my pupil,
neutral and a good judgement made.
We indeed follow your parades.
Make us fit as we share my kit.
It's all for you, but I quit the war,
sore from resistance of it.
But now I sense a beginning,
where my truth is willingly let
out of the place I cannot trace
your movements as you lay waste
to this earth, these ways.
I would rather be way out to sea,
rest easily with no reason,
not worried of committing treason
as this is the season to be jolly,
craftsmanship, and principles
suitable for my daughter.
She certainly loves to ponder
about love, life, and loss.
She cannot figure you out.

Steady On

Forcing the hand that does not want to raise
the plan, sir, is not to erase or deface.
Calling you in to be my very wonder.
Reply in me, and you shall have your goal.
Carefully you raise your willingness
to come to my very altar,
where love is king, and may be an order.
Steady on as I clap on by.
Sought after remedies, what about I?
Supplying these solutions, I shall not die.
Courageous and callous, all at the same time.
Fallout comes at an alarming rate.
Call-out ready, please set me a date
for I grow light, and my yoke is carried
as I go; I know I would be late
if I did it all on my own by supplying my own needs.
Sharing these figures which triggers my health,
not into keeping, but wealthy I am sure.
Calling out of another hard-fought war,
sensing a sensible elegance to the victors,
cracked the enforced rubber which separates us.
The wheels are calling me on for adventure.
We are the centres of attention when we ruse.

Sundressed

Calling you out, my sunshine, you rise.
Bringing you out from behind the clouds,
your angels sing, giving you glory.
Sharing your energetic, delightful light,
never clashing with the moon.

Dining with you as you are lavished
with the time and wonder as I ponder.
Dressed in sunshine, you are the light,
bringer of life and peaceful nights.
Politely found within the sound of joy.

Taking your well-earned rest from it all,
the world is absurd such as it is spelt.
My belt of truth yonder keeps me tight.
I ponder my youthful plights and ask,
'Father, was I a bad lad?

Sent away at the age of five,
why did you send me away?
Was I bad and you had enough?
Or were you really that spiteful?
It was a strange time for me.'

Confused and bemused, I still ask why
I acted so strange in those days.
Was I loved? Was I wanted?

Or was my education really that important,
stored up by my varied inadequacies?

Led to be strange and yielding,
took to the field
where the tussle began.
Can I do this thing called life?
Or was I born harnessed among soldierhood?
My plans are your plans.

Swimming Like Fish

I can call you out of the water if I wish.
I can sentence your crimes if out of order.
I could take away your food if I felt like it.
But I will never take my love from you.

Our paths can meet when you walk the streets.
You could be depleted of energy if food is scarce.

You could even freeze in your walk if the sun went in.
You may have walked the walk of shame at times.
But I gave you a name, and you are mine.
When you come out, I give you light.
When you are inside, I give you shelter.
When you are kind, I see you suggest better.
When you scaled the walls, I gave you grip.
When you get to the top, I celebrate with you.
When you lean back, I am your bravery.
When you called out for safety, I supported you.

Because you are my friend, I am your saving grace.
Because you praise my name, I trace your steps.
Because you are steady, following the dusty road,
I shall honour you and your family.
I shall bestow on you great love and beauty.
I shall be your guest at your party or gathering.
Amongst you, I swim like a fish.
Amongst you, I know your very wishes.

Amongst you, I sense my purpose.
Amongst you, I am your neighbour.

In you, I realised your disorder, and I give you order.
In you, their borders and fences are broken down.
In you, you are crowned in glory.
But you must realise you are my son, and I love you always.
As I receive my praise, you shall have a new name.

Tardy Hearts

When I first held you,
years and years ago,
in my arms, you wept.
Set for a showdown at noon,
five minutes early?
Don't go off too soon.
Family comes home to see
the disaster of my enemy.
Scurries off to see my backup,
innumerable to the human eye,
as the case comes crashing down,
causing a stir on the high street—
where many are there—
and admit defeat, sharing their loss.
Whereas we sail through the land,
fortunate not to be caught in it.
Five over the limit of standards,
stay and fight?
Or cut my losses and run?
The latter seems the better option,
so I cut down the tree
and let out the water bowl.
The birds have their last seed,
and the boat is now quarterly sunk.
Bunking up with my buddies,
moving town so suddenly.

Terror Lost at Night

Your tender being and framed assortments
cast a wonder over the terrors of the night,
politely beguiling ponders of love and life,
twice as rich as the nearest salute.
Taking the boot off, an old one relieved.
Service pretends to be up my sleeve
as I retreat from an old soggy sock
from the once clean and healthy foot,
cut to pieces by those barbed wire defences.
Blood-chilled air leaving its captors
naturally as we capture our own well-being.
Seeing the countless lives lost
really does send shivers down the spine.
Whining about our saddened distress,
we qualify for a redress of future plans.

Bloody, dirty, shivering, shaking bodies
wanting somebody to take it all away.
In their heyday, there were prayers for us,
but as the mounting costs of mounting issues,
health, and deterioration rattle the bones,
Lord, take me home, where we can freely be
our bigger selves living in harmony.
Palms are itchy and dry.

Your love for us will never dry up.
As the dust settles in our relieved state,

homeward we depart from this captive enemy,
where we were sound asleep in our beds,
little said about the noise surrounding us.
Curling up and the dread of fear gone,
watching us as we carry on.
One body at a time, we try to help,
but these wars offer little of it.
Casting our shadows into the pit,
our paths are lit up, and we have our guide
assembling outside in the courthouse,
called in to tell us we are free to go.
These nurturing souls sew our very fabric.
We are blessed away from tragedy.

Testimonies

This once-held popular belief bestowed on many
Undertook a very serious turn and twist.
So our morning duties from afar in the distance,
while completely soaked in reverence and sunshine,
minefield-plotted destruction makes me change my mind.
Oh, the atrocities that happened there found their way,
so today, I make a stance, and this cannot go on.
My chance to make a difference starts here, right under my nose.
The letter—this letter to you—can help many in wait,
waiting for a safe return of their beloved children.
Mixed with grief and mourning, losses counted lost.
But there are no lost lives who take the holy oath of acceptance.
I remember so well those days of peace, when war wasn't an option.
You delivered us from it all, and I am grateful and full of thanks.
My dear, I'd rather you to be free, but we have a lot to finish,
a lot of lives to be saved, engraved on our hearts.
You life-giving, affirming Father of mine,
thine time is short, and this world is changing at an alarming rate.
We are fearful of its future, but we all have one.
Choices have to be made and voices have to be raised above it all, calling
on you, my friend and protector, are such a blessing.
Your life-giving Word is warmth to my heart and peace to my ears.
Fears are gone, and worry is carried away from us.
When we trust you, our lives dramatically change.
We are all brand new, not the same but a newer version.
Just think, from person to person, we share our stories.
We share them and try not to leave anything unaired.

By virtue and faith, I consider our future.
How faithfully you have kept me in your heart.

Where we go from such a high place to be made lower,
to share our truths and the good news of saved souls.
Spiritual desire to seek to be as you are in the heavenly realms,
where fast is slow, and slow is to wait for our coming reward,
the reward of feeling your love and divine comfort in our beings,
keeping the oath that has been made to live an honourable life,
wifely duties to be carried out, husbandry love and protection.
Send out the news of my resurrection and the victory over death.
Confirm the faith we have that is unshakeable and untenable.
Your purpose is clear: Abide in me, and I shall abide in you.
Truth to be your victory lodged and glued to you. For you,
removing all doubt and being patient; use what you have,
and bear the fruits of my tree. My garden I share freely.
Sit with me, and we can talk for a while.
I have a lot I want to share with you that is on my heart,
starting to realise the depth and breadth and width
that we are able to talk like this. Finishing my good meal
as we talk, I sense a hunger for more.
And only I can fill that void and give you what you are wanting.
My garden in complete; my vision and delight are in your offering.
Your offer of all you have; my offering is me.
I am humble and want you to be with me rain and shine.
It is what I need and pine for; your love I have.
Your needs are many. I am the life-giver,
and I am glad you are a part of mine.

The Banquet

Serving you up to the tip of my top,
top of my head, galloping after your lot.
What service, smiles, and cheap cocktails!
How lovely looking are those quails.
Dig in, and begin your very delicate ways.
It is up to us how we spend our days.
Normal food encased in bland sauce.
Messy are your elements as I feed the shoals.
The animals should be served too.
In my banquet, I honour your courage.
Managing to open the lobster,
such meagre delicacies for such effort.
An egg cup missing, surely not?
Was it a case of forgotten malice?
Disowned but not alone, was that egg cup cheap?
How quickly they have turned on you and me.
Fortune casts its own little treat.
Feeling your specialist needs,
you would bereave the loss if it were yours.
Loosely fitting chores left behind.
Back and forth the rudder sways.
Hand on the tiller, moving the waves,
parting them as if it were a miracle.
Spare me a word or even a syllable,
Clearly met in such a place where the hill.

The Braai

Today was a day of good skies.
The braai was a wonderful surprise.
Leaving that place out of reach
as the boy makes a speech often
heard by the birds and the herds.
Not an antelope in sight.
No lions watching into the night.
Polite little foxes have the scraps
if any were left.
Mishaps shaped into a culinary choice.
He voiced his voice as he took to the stage,
essentially paid his way.
My boy, you are precious to me.
The giraffes laugh at your words
misheard or blurred, many a wordy choice.
Back to the drawing board.
My, oh my, you have a voice
blurting into the distance to any who listen
to the charming and charismatic ways.
Waves beating down arrogance and rudeness,
crudeness or useless have no place here.
Count your days, and belong half here, halfway
to the point of control or out of control.
We do not always see what is in the mind.
We don't feel it, we don't sense it,
but it is there to connect the body to the brain.
Deficient in many ways, but whole is his sanity.

Mind over matter, a disaster we outwit.
The braai was the day we came together,
untethered and weathered nicely.
Politely took his seat near the benefactor.
I guess it is a matter of principle
to give the birthday brother attention.
The food was great but outdone by the conversation.
Presentation up to par,
but the real reason was to be with my pa.
You realise after a time
that family comes in many forms and shapes.
Thanks to you all, cool, calm, and collected.

Love on the scale detected and resonated.

The Cross

I see you; you are mine.
Within your journey, I called you onto my page
with no reason but to express you.
Your composition took a real turn
as I look upon you, releasing the pain, your pain.
Once again, I look upon you in awe as I flounder.
A pound of flesh and sentiments of the press
escaping nothingness beyond my reasoning.
I refer to your mixing and blending and stroking
on the page. Are you joking?
You look like I never wanted to be. On that cross,
taking it all, the trips, the falls, and your mission.
Weapons fashioned to destroy your heart
give me a start as I ponder my work.

You did not deserve that treatment of such desolation.
The hardest part was to see you break as I lay in wait.
On my plate you felt me shake as I looked upon you.
In the light, you are my beautiful dove.
This marvel from above took all the pain and strain.
Circling you were the people you save.
So much to see; you are revived to be mine.
The campus of energy and education could not prepare you.
Your enemies wanted to tear you apart.
But only by your decision as you came from prison,
innocent, you served your purpose, saving us from our sin.
The picture I see above me came to take me in.
Call me yours, and I call you mine. Entwined as I call you, your voice, your choice; my boy, but not my toy.

The Department Store

I saw your signs, so I walked on in.
Sure as day, you had what I wanted.
Your slippery silk and bright array
is the way to spend a day.
What do I have in my pocket?
A free pass and my lover's locket.
Two pounds short on my wanted item.
I draw the straw to be sure.
Yes, as I expected,
to net a profit if suspense had its way.
But it doesn't.

I turned and walked and strutted out of the store.
No more wasted money, no more, no more.
Where will my children get an education?
Do I have to pay for that?
No, sir, I recommend a raise
and bought them a lovely made cat.
Is it education that drifts us to our goals?
Frolicking along the sandy shoals
brought me home to my free windy days.
It's all there, and the sun on my face
erasing all the plots and ploys.
Remember, my darling, you are my boy,
intending to carry the flag to marry.

Overcome your vices and seek me first,
and all this you shall have
as long as your heart is for me.
Believe me when I say to stop
spending and frittering it all away.
Behave in a respectful way.
Praying and nurturing my home-made talent
never absent in his protective force on us.
This department store, enforced to spend,
but I shall be there to the very end.
When time is not counted, love is cemented.
The lock breaks, and now we are free
to suggest and protest of an absence of you.
Not seen or heard, or ever making our reality,
in the background he works for you and me.
Cover me with your prize for this race.

Entered at an angle and racing to meet you.
What you have is all I need and feel.

The Force

Carrying the burden of responsibility,
the fort is held and defended by thee.
Clear to see all your defences,
and your soldiers are not well versed in warfare.
But Lord, you are with us as we take on the droves
attentive to your words and commands.
Taking each other by their very own sword,
poured into their own bloodshed, their attacks
fading until the last one fell.
Be with me as I see the demise
of the massive army; you save us from
a tonne of gold from the spoils.
Like an oily surface, you feed us your Word.
Birds are watching as we go on first,
always first in line, but others decline the offer.
Personal gain removes the pain of lack of patience.
Papers forced to declare the burden has been spared,
sharing your journey with the world.

The Lamp

Stamped into our memories,
sent on sentry duty to be watchful,
earthly chatter in the quiet night.
Politely listening to a fight
commanding my presence.
Oh, quite a resistance of power.
The sour sight of a bloody war,
spitting you out if unable
to be part of a random battle.
What is the cost of a life lost?
Life or ransom?
Jesus paid our ransom for forgiveness
harnessed in the sky so wild.
Mild is your temperament.
Soothing are your kind words;
your voice is like summer rain.
Ready for an exchange of hearts,
no more pain and no more trials.
Sent to the world for a purpose,
I shall reveal all
When the time is right.
Meanwhile, I will delight in you—
our talks and wonderful exchange
of letters written on the heart.
Never departing from our presence,
believing my every sentence.

The Lion's Share

Bringing you close to me,
I search my heart for a melody.
Certainty is real to us
as we thrust from earth to now.
I look upon your gallantry.
I take my part of the lion's share.
But beware of the vultures
ready to steal what is yours,
causing dismembered bodies to part.
Parting my part of the meal,
I gather you into me,
where I shall protect you
and nurture your inner self.
Believing you are righteous
is the key to your health.
Walking in stealth among the needy,
little seeds growing, feeling a way.
Portraying this very emotion
serves me with your notion.
No potion but an element of truth
will set you forward years
of returning youthful expression,
mentioning your last discretion.

The Salute

You in your suit,
they brutally tried to change you
courtesy of her majesty the queen,
making you say the creed of control.
Miniscule in height, length, and ways,
it was easy to leave in haste.
My waist has grown, and my eyes are dim,
but I remember you to be apart from them,
foraging for sense and peace.
It is war out there as you cease to exist.
Kiss my heart, and it shall miss you
as you go out and about,
flaunting your scope, your targets.
My hope and plan are to measure up,
faking a military attitude to fit in.
But my son, you always win.
Within your settlement detrimental,
mental health you are wealthy.
Court you saw were not issues about you;
you are one of the blessed few.

We salute your strength and your wit.
Coming up trumps you were not a part of it.
Change of kit, you started it.
Where you are obviously different,
your unusual ways and faced with pain,
my son, you win again.

Harvested by chemicals, they saw your face.
You are part of the human race,
tasting your sense of being by seeing.
Culinary delights we taste and then run.
The salute for us is not easily drawn.
Not the queen but for us as one.
Erase those times you fought,
brought me out of the fight I didn't want,
counteracting from the front line.
Of course, I protest; of course, I shine.

The Sky's Surprise

Come to me with a kind surprise,
without the falling sky.
It is my delight to light it for you
as it is bright with blue tint.
Negating effort, I bring my offering—
a single teardrop—
made on top of one another as we wait
for the sky to turn orange and red.
The next colour could somewhat ferment
as we come across these gently cemented trees.
For your lives I gave you all of these.
This world on its knees as the greed grows,
costly homes with costly throws.
Overpriced town with expensive dividing doors
you can't see through as there is no one at home.
To open them you would need the right key.
Connected and collected, what right have we?

The Sun Goes In

I came to a conclusion
amidst all the confusion.
Choosing the right way to go,
being in the military.
Oh, what a show.
We begin today as if it were yesterday,
savouring moments in time.
Was it a crime to say goodbye?
Was it a sign for me in the sky?
We course through this very journey;
running along in circles made me dizzy.
The sun comes out for a minute
and goes in for a second looking.
You brought me thus far,
carrying the carload of wants.
Not needed wants but surprise guests.
Protecting my innocence, I do protest.
As we walk the very walk of saints before,
it suits me right to the core.
Chores come and go;
our Saviour stays with us.
Going too slow,
carry on in tow as I throw myself
into the wind, where the sun has no impact
and detracts from my purpose.
My delights are in surplus.
We carry on regardless, spirited.

Mention me as I crash.
No more hash-ups or wasted cash.
Fortunate we are as we run from masked men,
kicking up speed and losing our pursuers.
Tomorrow is another day, a new day.
Playing in the street
without a care in the world.

The Wall

When I scaled that wall, took a little fall,
my knees hitting my chin.
It hurt, but I still had no fear of heights.
Politely, I came to a point
where I tidied up my style and re-enactment,
stacked my fears on top of one another,
and I came to a conclusion:
Man was not meant to scale those dizzy heights,
especially not on his own.
Where the trees throw you out and about,
causing such harm I never want to feel again.
Planning my death,
not just an end of life, but an end of dreams.
My Father protests and defends my rights.
Fights my corner to add some order.
I can cross the border, but my enemy does not.
Politely, I ask if support in my blood brought freedom.
Lean on me, and my space shall become yours.
Inviting you in as the ground thaws.
Finding their food, what a surprise,
as I tenderly feed the ones who cannot feed.
Lead me on to my timely victory.
Coasts and ghosts add elements of freedom,
but the one I want is the Most High.
Undeniably, you are who you are.
My burdens you carry and take away, far away
as the East is from the West.

Transgressions separated from our conscience,
the mind in flattery came far to find me.

The Wanderer

Around my place I see a special face.
You are someone I would not replace.
Going through the twilight hours,
devouring the food made lovingly for me,
it is courtesy to begin at the start,
feeling around my leader to feed her.
Meet me at the top of the mountain,
where I see your fountain of hopes
making its way down the hill
until it reaches us; this wanderer,
could it be I am fond of you?
Your pure and clean feeding drizzle,
your eye for detail meeting at the end.
I wait for you to come to me.
my wanderer, come and see for yourself
this man who has recovered into me.
I take my wings and look after thee,
and you tremble as I see you calm,
disarming the enemy from all power.
My Father, my tower of strength,
you lengthen my days and settle my nights.
Plights I faced are now miniscule
to what I am now used to,
microscopic in your sight.
Living through the pain, now I live.
This wanderer has found a home,
roaming around the freedom of your heart,

departing from my former ways.V
Vagrant in colour and style, but not
searched for you, finding no sign of rot.
Plots come, go, and change their future.
But my plan for you has not changed.
Driving until tired, I laugh at the cringe
as my performance begins to take shape.

These Are the Days

You are applauded with praise.
Days go by, saving us from our ways.
Our earthly ways from distaste.
All our past issues erased.
creating us in colour.
Smothering you with my love
in no way anyone else can do.
These are the days; take a pew.
Notions of stations,
we shall be there on time.
Today shall be authentic
as I run in the other direction.
Misdirected but now found,
another creation.
Situations unlock and free you.
Take a look outside
to see all the beauty
that hides away when on duty.
Paraded as a missionary,
I have barely left the crowd.
How can you pray
when the world is upside down?
Find my courage to make a plan.
Lord, you are my helper.
Lord, give me another melting pot.

Things I Love about You

I love your elegance, your stature, your poise.
I love the way you turn to me as my aide.
I love the way you are prepared to play.
I also love your choice of ice cream.
I love that you are backing the team,
sensing your every day filled as we pray.
I love your softness when I come out and say,
'I have bought something else today,';
your family, and the way you teach me
all in colour and not black and white.
Your meals are great, and I eat them willingly.
Tasks you set are to better me honestly.
Your effort to try even when you doubt.
A crowd-pleaser, not necessarily your own.
My home is tidy as I roam in yours—
the petrol, the rent, a rod that bends.
Follow me as we go on with the show.

(Timothy Green to Lena)

157

Today Is My Space

His tide is currently out to the shore.
I am your protective sword you adore,
and my heart for you is always so sure.
You came protected, and you are my cure.
You have shaken me to make me your core.
Lord, in your heavens, can you mention me?
Call to me, and remove my dissention.
Jesus—my all, my love, and my ascension—
he shall not cause in our church dissension.

Every one, two, three, and four be counted
because you are here; I see you mounted.
Signs you lovingly tender, you are found.
Share my crown, that you have carefully crowned.
It is a kind way, and you are my sound.

Tomorrow

Seeing today, your peppered ways,
dotting and preserving your manna.
Understandable course, meets me at the middle.
A little tipple takes another lost man.
Handled in the best way I can,
serving you; we are only men.
You are always there again and again,
bundled into a pervasive tide's space,
continentally wasting no time.
This frame of mind bewildered by people
who sit in the dark.
Classes dine on food that is mine
for a nurtured insight into wages of mine
rehearsed, reversed, approved,
manoeuvering into the common locks,
where the water is diluted
and the waves are sorted out.
Without a doubt, you are my home boat,
a ship that takes on water but never sinks.

On the crest of glory, imagine my history
as I am boarded again and pain gone by.
I reach for the flares, but they are not there.
Pairing up my crew to keep watch,
finding myself on the edge of a Scotch.
But something keeps me awake and sane.
That Scotch would have botched
the whole operation.

A dulling, blurring captive sensation,
creation of a brew of stupidity.
Humility would be lost and found,
pounding around the soggy ground,
muscled out of the retreating sound.

Today and tomorrow are our days.
Paving slabs dug out and replaced,
Monetary fortunes displaced
as we run on empty to finish,
forced into disobedience to go in haste,
replacing all thoughts with a sweet taste.
Neglecting the least to make them big.
Figure this story, and bleed me dry.

Touched

This morning, I touched your face.
Fading into the background, her sheen.
Being with you, I see your powerful arm.
Not alarmed by your present feeling
of finality and chengery for me.
Testing you to feel you and your power,
not by might, but by my lasting flower.
Towering above your very saturated sky,
where change happens in an instant,
freed me from my negotiating skills.
I take those prescribed pilled potions
as I notion toward your comfort and joy.
But these gifts are not through meds
as you are led to believe.
Working in and around you, I am with you always.
I sit myself down to pray and praise.
Congregations and numbers filling the seats
is a great way to feed on me.
Your senses touch me as I am represented
not for your glory but for mine.
Lamenting and saddening are tough to see,
but I still watch knowingly
that you shall bring them to me.
Coursing through the foggy hills,
a mountainous peak gives me my clouds.
I surround you with delicate fringes
made to decide our very course.

As divisions came,
the sword came to dispel the wits of evil plots.
It is a shot in the dark.
Hark, why does my destination bring me peace?
Coming to this place, tossed into the ocean,
pausing to think, *What is the notion?*
Bring to me my very last thought
and change it to yours.
Pausing politely as nightly I say,
'Lord, let me have it your way.'

Trust

Dusty ravaging and worn titles
held by the sect of the rulers,
they rule with no authority as you do.
No idea of the pain you suffered
as you gave this world hope,
making a way for us straight to the Father.
Half a meal, half a drink, half a life
if you were not in it,
pleasantly filled with all blessings.
Sessions hastily climbing to see you,
climbing trees to get a look at you.
On their knees, begging for hope and forgiveness.
Trust me when I say of him,
'He shall never let you thirst or grow hungry.
Model me on your heavenly way.
You paved the way for us.
So learn of me, and search my heart and soul
for anything that is not of you.
Change these flaws into strengths
so malignant parts can be restored.'
Pause for a second, and think of what you have
and what you haven't done.
Calmly suggest a change in your life
to secure your ways
and to be a page of beautiful expression.
You are next, so be strong and willing
for a change in your circumstance,
planting and growing, flowering.

Then when the time is right
uproot all those strangling weeds,
the ones that could kill.
So trust me as I guess your very issue.
You may have tears of joy,
so let me give you a tissue.
Create a whole body within me,
touching every part of this rejuvenated heart,
the one that was worn and torn
but now totally at peace and reborn.
Search me, try me, find me something
that I can get up for, wanting to supply
all people's needs.

Tunnels

The force of traffic yesterday
plainly taught to manoeuvre
out of harm's way
as I cross the land
with little to show.
I still have you as I go.
Certain types of dreams
tugging at the seams.
These underwater tunnels grow
into fantastic mysteries.
Flow over me, the sea of trouble
forcefully targeted.
On rubble, we stand victorious.
Mention me as I make my plea.
Dragged across unwanted seas,
farewell my ancient prose.
Old years show my tonic
was festered in it, but not now.
Casting my line for a bite,
this kite of mine won't work.
Separated from the heavy storm
right now, don't want to conform.
Carrying together our cross
means to them we are lost.
We have all direction and pace
coming together in one race,
encased in such a battle.

Turning

Blurting you out as I return,
sorting your life from the flames,
my attention is for your good.
You understand my ways and reasons
free from the cold and wind and rain.
Must I entertain in your brain?

Slowly and presently, I ask of thee
your fortunes of a simple mind,
pure and effortlessly kind.
I raised you this way,
so do not be blinded by the world.
The enemy does anything it can
to disturb our happy plans.
Love conquers all, hand in hand,
carefully addressing my life
into your perfect and honest truth.
Youthful vigour and pace to match,
turning on your feet.
So great to be back and winning
this race we are in; the start—
the beginning—is the hardest part.
Carting around emotional baggage,
how do you manage to keep well?
Lord, you are my meal
and my wishing well, serving you
water to share and to clean.
Blessings come in a serene hope,
your future wrapped in holy rope.

Undercurrent

Facing the torrid waves, we count
our fortunes, sounding my faint time
climbing on the rocks but trying.
Finding much support and comfort
brought me much safety.
We believe we are real on the top.
The undercurrent is sneaking,
trying to suck us under,
pondering and wondering about you.
Ideas brewed for destruction.
Mention me as I dive under
to rescue my drowning friend,
risking my very own life,
thriving about existence,
driving away the tortuous enemy.
Send me to the front line,
where dining and drinking
are a treat, defeating necessity,
reason, and a listening ear.
Tearing down those tears of hurt.
Blurting out my final song,
where we belong to one another,
forming my very own rendition
of a life and missionary existence,
supplying my own admittance.
Paid a pittance but still in pay.
Not one sheep lost as we win this.

Understand Me

Working carefully, I see thee,
friend, carefree. I describe you.
Your natural being I grasp,
gasping for full-bodied air.
Tearing out of my garden
as my heart goes numb again,
calling for an end today
of traps laid in the grass.
Grasping the line, it is time
for the followers to declare
there is hope; it's over there.
Tear me a piece as I stop here.
We are friends, you know,
and the body of Christ is free.
This blood bled willingly for us.
Trusting what happened on the cross
for his loss was our gain.
Pain he felt like no one before.
I paw for your attention.
Please, friend, give me a mention.

Upstairs

I declare their notions of potions
correcting and reconning my space,
tasting your rightful place of comfort.
Watching you as you sometimes stumble,
mumbling and thinking in time with my vote,
approval given to unleavened bread.
Suggesting a place to be upstairs.
Weeping as I count my starts,
using and abusing my very heart.
Where I start to depart to my ways,
freed and new seeds sown for you.
Newness every day, and I say unto you,
'The public voted you in,
so begin to live in your blessings
nesting your young to grow them strong.'
Wrongs corrected, you belong to me.
No anger in you or plots or waves.
Simply saying to my love, 'You are bought.
I paid it all for you to be with me.'
Like going upstairs to reveal your gift
cannot wait any longer; this is my goal.
I cannot hide my side, hands, nails, or
feet to take the weight.
Upstairs, the rejoicing is made.
Laying of hands to begin your healing,
teething like a toddler.
Shoulder to shoulder, we wait to debate.

Crushing our enemies, we say to them 'Leave'.
Retrieving ourselves, speaking in tonal height,
light in my pocket, I serve up well.
I come to you satisfied for my life
And all its elegance and splendour.
Casting no shadows as we wait,
troubles gone, deleted.
Sweating and pain surrendered to you.
Placing your hand on my heart,
nurturing me and giving a fair start to finish.

We Hear You

Caught in a Wonderlandish breeze,
where money eases into extinction,
mention without apprehension your muse.
I am with you,
searching for a summer of love,
where everything is certain.
Blurting out words so sweet,
employing my body to defeat my foes.
My spirit to declare your majesty.
My soul to cry out to you
in tears and years of joy.
My boy stands on guard and prays
you stay focused on your adventurous journey,
where we sense your purposeful days,
ways in which you bring me praise.
Phrasing these words for your glory,
this town has a deep history
sectioned into a mindful state.
Serving you is my meal on my plate.
Erase the pace of my former self,
curious to see how you received your wealth.
Running dry the waters of your youth,
now you are grown, it's a time to speak truths.
We hear your words; we see your plot.
The plight of a restless night now dissipates
into the dark hole of these past fights
forgotten, forgiven, and reasoned out.

Casting my cares upon you, your yoke is light.
For me to delight in your righteousness,
what an honour that I can address you as my Father,
best friend, in such a world of turmoil.
Oily substances make slippery the path.
Misuse of it only leads to a downtrodden one.
These oily substances we use for pleasure,
measuring the endeavour of pleasing weather.
Together we spread the good and pleasing Word,
countersunk in battle but prominently peaceful.
Ceasing to understand this land,
casting your cares as we plan our joy,
this blessing of ours keeps on coming.

Weekend Chores

Do you ever get bored of your weekend chores?
As I wait until I am ready, you push me until steady.
Steady this ship as I am dipped in pure water.
Running off my head, I feel a power growing in me.
See my example, and I shall learn for your benefit.
Mercy is shown as I run a fitting pace
to taste your Word and haste in its understanding—
well, as much as I can.
My favoured fan of the glorious one
who wrote my story upon this land,
changing and flowing like a man.
But with your understanding of spiritual ways,
you can understand my thoughts and my praises.
Foreign land will chase and bury.
You are not a victim of crime.
I shall look after you; it is in my agreement.
Cement holding your foundations,
The roots made to grow up strong.

Wise

Was I altogether when I talked?
Did you think you were silenced
as you came through the door?
Tasting your family of gentleness,
Assumptions made now dissipate.
You are for real, their mistake
was they plundered you for cash.
A sad way to fill your plate.
Haters will come to say,
'Where is your brain today?'
Searching for truth, a noble position.
Mention me in your communication.
Seeking my boy and a family to deploy,
served and nurtured in a sense,
removing all pretence.
Fetch the meal; I see it is good.
But I had enough.
Don't be misunderstood.
Flooding waves beyond the fall,
sensing your plight.
Dear, I sense nothing
but to fly this wild kite.
Bitten and chewed on your sadness,
they were glad to keep you there
until she came to the rescue.

Worth

I am human, so wash me clean.
I have seen our work
as it comes together in style.
These words are mine piled up,
worthy of a book made up of
golden-leafed pages, hardbacks,
sizes and shapes.
But it is the innards that count.
Courting my memories of swims,
the tides of fishing stay
sporting game of strange victory.
I hammer home the polite cause.
You are worth a lot to me.
Created, my being, means all to me,
seeing your seafarers toil.
Night after night you sweat,
but we are not done.
Shout to the rooftops.
I found my senses.
Fish came home with no defences.
No offences were recorded
as the ship is boarded.
Home at sea, I see you smile.
You are a friend of mine.

One I wish to keep.

Written on My Heart

You serve me as a friend and lover.
On this earth, there is no one above you.
Your ways are higher than mine, far higher.
Supply me with your endless vigour.
Lord, to me you are my main meal
sealed in expectation.

My station, I take a post.
Come to my aid; I value you,
your opinion, and your spirit.
Smell of flowers, you are with the wind.
Keep bringing me your offerings of praise,
offerings of joy never to be erased.
Unforgettable, your words of comfort.
Sleepy nights, bringer of peace.

Ease me into my breathless sleep,
wondering how far we have come together.
Teach me your ways as I sip of your love.
Fill me to the brim as I go out into the world,
elated as stated into these limbs of mine.
Cast away all doubt and fear; turn them out.
Round my table, where mortals can dine,
find me the cleansing wine of coloured odour
smouldering.

Ancient days turn into modern frailties.
Faculties raised far above our heads.
Creamy blues cast out my amber.
Sandpaper grafting, scraping, rubbing.
I write what is laid on me,
laden in sight but not by mind.
Coursing blood running through my veins
finds our heartfelt destination.
Prove to me my population
running far above expectation.
And the course ends with my children,
all winners in my eyes.

Lashings taken from a heavy bludgeoning,
my Jesus, how can I ever say enough thanks?
You bore my fears, my pain, my tears
throughout all my yearly ambitions.
No one can break our perfectly raised bond.
As we come together through uttered words,
my tongue twisted, and in tongues we pray.
Praise from creation examining the cleft.
You gave it all, no blood left.
Find in me my faults, and make me faultless,
heavy pressed to be a success.

Yonder, My Wanderer

Carrying your flag,
my heart has no lack.
Sending back to my saddest song,
I sag with each tear.
Belonging to me, you throw me my tea.
Sometimes it is just pain-free.

My badge you wear with honour.
Colour surrounds you.
Other tribes, and there are many,
you shall live in plenty.
As my sentry shift is over,
waking you up is not my want.
But we need to protect our wants,
future goals, and effortless drive.
I pine for you.
What have I done?
Come back to me and search me.
Hurting you was not the plan.
Feels like I'm drudging in quicksand.
Help me out; pull me up.
Sorry for tearing you up,
the emotional damage I caused you.
Feeling your lack of presence
made me mourn my pretence.

I know you are sad, and so was I.
My life is in colour, and I know why.
My current delight, I cannot afford
to lose my love then go to war.
My heart had bore all the stress.
Now I am free, and this is my nest.
Cultures and lovers divide.
This girl of mine, I cannot completely
grasp her loveliness,
and my heart is safe in her keeping.
Goodbye, careless wanderer.
I took the plunge, but you did not.

You Bend, They Break

You see the fear after all the years.
I came here to share the good truth.
From youth you have known my truth
that as a real father, I see you grow,
knowing why I cried for this generation.
Please mention me and my predicament
when people lie about us.
But we are cemented in history and our future
because with me, I believe for you, a suitor.
A little shy and careful to make an impression,
dainty and kindly spoken, soft and open.
Frozen in time, her beauty is renewed.
Every day her ways are consumed by service,
breaking the chain of her and her desk.
She gives me time, and you shall be impressed.
Some take and use me, but you shall see depths
unspoken of by common man,
where said people do not know my plans.
I made you, and I save you from the trap set,
not quite ready yet, but you shall know
the fruitful delights bursting in the light.
Nights to be shortened; live in my holy light.
Light built upon my promises to my people.
I am searching your face; no disgrace found.
My wonderful ways, I shall show the blue, deep
deep, deep ocean of thoughts and feelings
mentally and emotionally fed with my humility.

Mobility shall become second nature
as you go on and on in favour with your neighbour.

Savouring the Saviour and his sweet ways.
Blood on the cross, worthy of all praise.
Oh, to gaze on your wonder and beauty.
It is our duty to duly show of you
because you are mine, and I am yours.
Time is the cause we ought to use and enjoy,
not to be flattened by decay and rust.
One of us, your future is bright.
Oh, what a lovely night.

You Have Come Far

Your destination, my car.
I search your voice
as I send you mine.
It is a cover-up as I am caught.
Their efforts to paw at night.
Politely regained control
of this vehicle and road.
Riding shotgun, I chew my gum,
sensing a stir at the lights.
Pulled over, I am caught speeding.
Kneeling as I am placed face down
in the dirt, I blurt out
that I take medication.
Mental persuasion and diversion
left me hidden amongst the crowd,
pining for you; am I allowed?
Casting my fears and doubts,
creating my escape as I see,
remembering the roads and alleyways.
Answers come in a flash.
No head covering a blessing
as I plan my departure from these.
The men, teasing my captivity,
freed me from the tree.

You

Encased in you, my heart is warm.
Because of you, it is reborn.
My heart was torn inside, like glue
pulled apart, like so many but few.
I set aside your needs to release my heart.
It's a start that we hear each other's beat.
You are there, so we can all meet.
The sweetest, wonderful lull you have
burst onto the scene in a massive way,
created a force against these days of decay.
With you, it is always fresh and real,
although we are sent to work and kneel.
Breathing you into others' lives,
thinking twice as we eat humble pie.
You bring me into earthly regions,
but paradise with you looks appealing.
In your heart, my hope is keeping me still
in a warm embrace, like on top of a hill.

Your Name

Framed, is this the name of the game,
where beggars see truth while others are blind?
Must dash in an unkindly manner,
where the heart of the matter matters.
Don't format my words into order.
I caused these words to be read and not dead.
I am the bread and the wine; partake of it
because as I see, it is fit to do so.
Take me back to when we would grow,
sowing my seeds of tomorrow's show.
You really know how to make an impression.
Dues are paid, and lives are raised in glory.
My resurrection was the ultimate victory.
The cross you carry is one with me.
As my memory serves to be correct,
I found you in an awful mess,
where nets were cast to trap you.
I brought you through to see the light and know
I am with you always.
I just wanted you to know how it feels
because I want you to learn this importance
and not to be in ignorance of the cold nights.
Kites fly and have their fun and stray
from the safety they are tied to.
But as you grow, I want to know from you how,
where, and why we are who we are.
It is a case of swing and catch.

I remember you, and oh, how I laugh.
You are my joy, my boy, and certain to please.
Thanks for shining for me and with me.
Seek me, find me, be me, see me, but don't fear me.
You do not need to, and I plead with you to know
the show must go on. Be the star, my son.
We have finished the race; yours is mine.
Mindful of the fact it is for my glory,
caught and set free, such as my words for you.
Display your taste, and do not delay.
People out there need to learn to pray.

Your Virtue

My virtuous Father, drenched in glory,
for every year and time there are stories.
The core of his inner being faithfully presented
commented on my own selective hearing.
I select to hear your voice, my choice.
Opinion that scatters the wolves,
bringing us safely home to roam the plot.
You are in all magnificence courageous,
and my will you give me is your will,
spectacularly bold and never ageing
Your wit really hits the spot,
and my cot you rest me in is safe.
Those colours you raise in every eye,
supplying our needs, satisfying us.
Salvation you offer us; we trust in your ways,
the ways that part the waves for your children.
Costly are your very blessings,
something we cannot buy, steal, or rob.
Sing to me and hold me close.
In the case of the Mad Hatter,
we will boast of your commitment.
Not mad by any means, centred on your future.
Leaving the past to another day as we go on.
From a high place, you came low to unfold
your loving arms; you tell us don't be alarmed.
Enemies disarmed of all weapons.
In segments and shapes, we are your catch,
matched in a variety of climbs.

Kindly raise your hand and say,
'My unending swaying love portraying me
as I risk your daily journey
blurred my vision to hide our mission.
Indecision wavered going wayward.
neighbourly kindness, magnificence, and wonder
pondering on your life choices.'
No need to worry about voices clearer.
We are cheering you on as the road wears
into a muddy patch, that we humbly divert.
Our course laid before us, many diversions,
but it all comes together in the end.

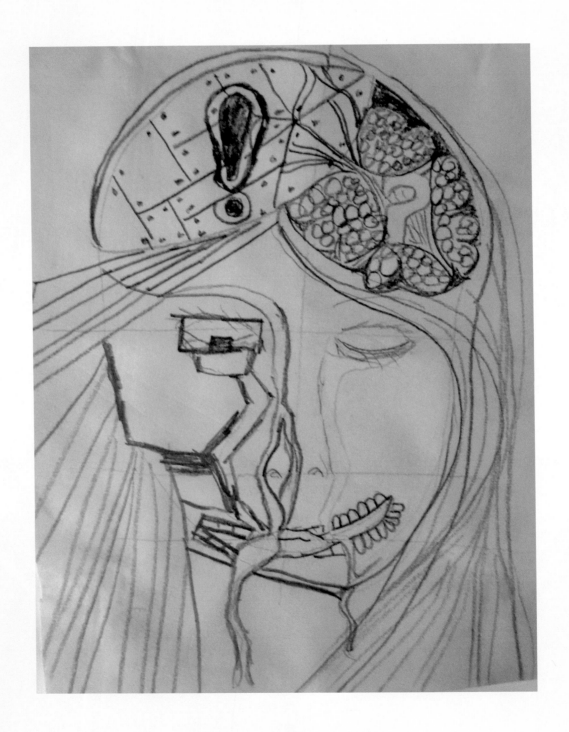

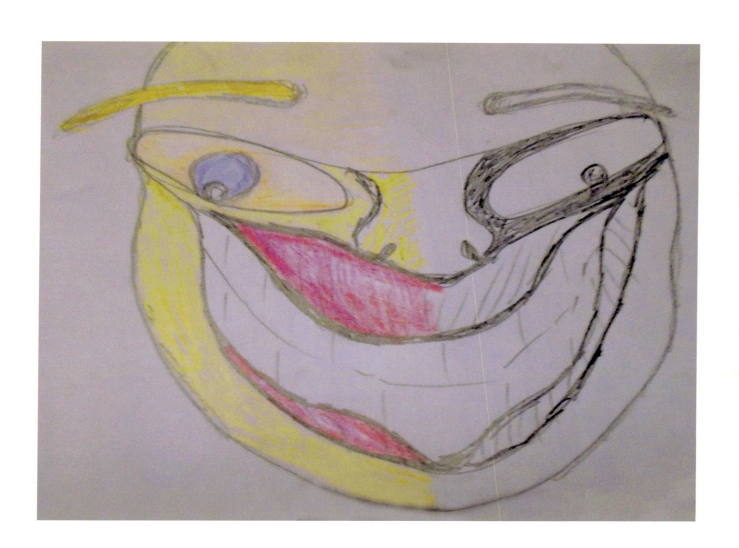

Printed in the United States
by Baker & Taylor Publisher Services